# OVERVIEW

**Overview**

One of people's primary needs is social interaction. By communicating well face-to-face, we build healthier and more productive relationships, work more effectively, and gain more satisfaction from life. However, communicating well is a skill that requires learning and practice. It isn't something that people intuitively know how to do well.

To communicate well, both you and your listeners need to understand and trust one another. Communication is defined as the transmission or sharing of ideas, thoughts, or feelings between people. The verb communicate originates from the Latin root communicare, which means to share or make common.

All communication is a two-way process. Information is not only given by one person, but also received and understood by another. Interpersonal communication is communication that occurs specifically between small numbers of participants, usually face-to-face.

This means that participants are able to share information not only through words but through sight and sound too. In the context of interpersonal communication, participants can give immediate feedback, which may not necessarily be verbal. For example, a person could nod to show agreement or understanding.

The quality of interpersonal communication has a crucial role to play in the success of any organization. It directly affects the quality of an organization's decision making, problem solving, and relationships. So good communication is essential for an organization and its employees to act effectively.

**Organizational success**

It's difficult for any organization to succeed if its employees can't communicate skillfully because communication impacts so many factors within an organization. When information is shared with employees in a positive and skillful way, it boosts productivity and profitability, giving meaning, motivation, and a personal context to people's work. When communication is poor or absent, employees may feel mistrustful, alienated, or less motivated to do a good job.

**Decision making**

Being able to give and receive accurate and comprehensive information is essential for decision making. Poor communication typically leads to poor decision making. Decisions made without discussion harm morale. Most decisions have to be considered within the context of how they will affect others. So stakeholders need to be consulted skillfully in order to bring their true opinions and insights to light.

**Dealing with problems**

Ineffective communication can give rise to mistakes, sometimes with very serious consequences. Many problems are prevented by an open, trusting atmosphere in which employees have the confidence to voice their doubts and questions.

**Relationships**

Poor interpersonal communication harms relationships between people in an organization, causing stress and mistrust. The result is that important information may be lost, distorted, or concealed. Negative criticism, gossip, or breaches of confidence can also cause lasting damage to organizations and to people. Good communication creates good working relationships, resulting in innovative, enthusiastic people who enjoy working together and who empower one another to succeed.

**Effectiveness**

Good communication conveys information that people need to know to be effective. It encourages good feedback, enabling employees to meet their goals more effectively. If communication within an organization doesn't allow people to give and receive feedback safely, ineffective behavior is not checked, and problems tend to mount.

Good communication and confidence go hand in hand. As your confidence rises, your communication improves. So many of the techniques for developing confidence also play a significant role in improving interpersonal communication.

**Benefits of confident communication**

Good communication is a skill. This means that it can be learned and should be practiced, like any other skill. Becoming an effective and confident communicator can be a lifelong process of learning and practice. It can also bring many satisfying rewards. As your communication skills improve, your relationships with others are enhanced. You are more likely to be understood, and you become far more effective. Interactions become more fun and more authentic. Good communication can bring real depth and meaning to your conversations with people.

This book covers several areas that will help you become a more confident communicator:
- key elements needed for confident communication,
- how to build trust, credibility, and rapport,
- how to prepare for communication,
- how to use your voice confidently, and,
- how to use body language to project confidence.

Joseph Baker, the CEO of a web design company, receives this e-mail message from Paul, the team lead on one of the company's design teams: "The client keeps delaying, but we can't do any further work without the CBG. I'm afraid we're going to miss Tuesday's deadline unless we get this."

The members of Paul's team understand the message because they're familiar with the context surrounding it. But it's likely to annoy a busy CEO like Joseph. Why has it been sent to him? Which client does it refer to? What is being delayed? What is a CBG? And, what does Paul actually want him to do? To find out, Joseph is going to have to give Paul a call.

Now consider a more targeted version of the message from Paul: "For the hospital web site project, we're still missing the client's corporate branding graphics – although we've been asking for them daily. Could you perhaps speak to the hospital's marketing director about this? If we don't get the graphics, we're going to miss our Tuesday deadline for the project."

Now it's clear to Joseph what the problem is and what he's being asked to do about it. The revised version is more likely to get results because it's targeted to the CEO.

Good interpersonal communication is essential, both in your personal and professional relationships. Interpersonal communication is the verbal and nonverbal interaction between individuals.

It includes skills like listening, questioning, and giving feedback. Good interpersonal communication skills facilitate better working relationships, which contribute to a better work environment. Conversely, poor interpersonal communication can lead to unsatisfactory relationships, lower morale, and misunderstandings.

Because situations vary, there's no such thing as a "one-size-fits-all" approach to communicating well. Instead, your approach should depend on the context for each communication. For example, what's the purpose of your message? Who is the intended receiver and what does this person need in order to understand your message? And what is the situation surrounding your message?

Communication is a complex process that includes many components. Good interpersonal communication depends on your ability to recognize and consider each of these components.

In this book, you'll learn about the key components of interpersonal communication and how they can influence the communication process. You'll learn about analyzing the needs and priorities of the intended receiver as an important step in preparing a targeted message, and about planning the context for delivering your messages to ensure they're as effective as possible.

You'll also learn strategies for delivering targeted messages and ensuring they're understood, and for getting useful feedback after your messages have been received. With the knowledge you gain in this book, you'll be equipped to communicate more effectively in all situations. Both at work and in your personal life, this can improve your relationships with others and enhance your success.

Imagine two ballroom dancers who forget that dancing is a partner sport, in which one person leads and the other follows. If they stop taking note of one other and focus only on themselves, the dance will break down and its meaning will be lost.

Think of communication as a dance. To do it well, you have to be able to follow and respond to the other person, rather than only pursuing your own agenda. What this means in practice is that being a good listener is just as important as being a good speaker. You might be a persuasive and articulate speaker. But if you don't listen – and listen well – the communication process may go awry.

Most people don't realize how easy it is not to listen well. In fact, people generally absorb only about a quarter of what they hear. This is because real listening takes effort. Listening involves more than just keeping quiet. It also involves actively engaging with the speaker – asking questions when necessary and showing that you understand.

We listen for all sorts of reasons – and the way we listen changes according to what we're listening for. Types of listening include informative, relationship, appreciative, critical, and discriminative listening.

### Informative

You probably find that listening to understand or learn is the kind of listening you practice most often. So you listen to gain important information that you need to fulfill your own goals. For example, you listen to the weather or traffic reports, to instructions, or to briefings and explanations.

### Relationship

You listen to your friends, colleagues, and family to show you care about them and to take part in their lives. This is relationship listening. You do this because others need to talk and may need your advice or opinion.

### Appreciative

Sometimes you listen to someone because of who that person is. You may do this if the speaker is someone you respect or admire, someone who inspires you, or someone you find comforting to listen to.

### Critical

A large part of our day-to-day listening is critical listening. You listen to people's arguments, debates, explanations, or excuses so that you can judge these yourself.

### Discriminative

Discriminative listening involves listening for more than just the facts – you also want to "hear" the speaker's underlying motives, intentions, or emotions. You do this by being sensitive to the nuances in the speaker's message.

No matter why you're listening, if there's a reason to listen at all, there's a reason to listen properly. Otherwise, you'll miss out on information that may prove vital.

Listening can be just as powerful as speech. If you meet someone who is well liked and charismatic, you've probably met a good listener.

Remember that what other people have to say is just as important as what you have to say to them. As an active listener, you approach each new conversation as an opportunity to learn something worthwhile.

There are several goals of effective listening:
- to listen attentively, in order to understand the speaker,
- to confirm your understanding to the speaker,
- to encourage full communication of the speaker's message, and
- to remain nonjudgmental and empathetic toward the speaker.

In this book, you'll learn why listening effectively is so important – and so difficult to get right. You'll learn how to recognize and overcome the barriers to effective listening. And you'll learn how to give a speaker your full attention and demonstrate that you understand.

By end of this book, you'll have a good grasp of the active listening technique and be well on your way to being an effective listener.

Suppose a colleague asks you to help her fix her computer, which has given her problems the whole day. She's running late and fears she won't be able to finish her presentation by the end of the day. Fixing her computer isn't your job, and you yourself are working frantically to complete an assignment on time. How do you react?

If you're able to say "no" politely and not to feel guilty because you honestly don't have time to help, you're behaving assertively. If you agree to help because this is simply the easiest approach and you'd feel guilty if you didn't, you're displaying passive behavior. Getting angry or annoyed that your colleague even asked for help when you're clearly busy is aggressive behavior.

**Question**

Typically, behaving assertively has more positive results than behaving either aggressively or passively.

How do you rate your own assertiveness?

**Options:**

1. Excellent
2. Good
3. Poor

**Answer:**

Option 1: It's great that you're generally assertive, but you should be careful not to behave aggressively. This book will cover how to behave assertively while maintaining respect for others and good relationships with your coworkers.

Option 2: Perhaps you struggle to behave assertively in certain situations. This book will cover how to behave assertively – even in difficult situations such as confrontations and disagreements.

Option 3: This book covers how to behave more assertively and how to approach different situations with your new assertive behavior.

Being assertive isn't only about standing up for your own rights – it's also about communicating more clearly and honestly. So assertiveness is a quality of good interpersonal communication, which is crucial for maintaining good relationships and getting things done effectively in the workplace.

It's not always easy to be assertive, and it can be especially difficult in certain situations. This book will teach you how to apply assertive behavior in four types of difficult situations:
- when you're disagreeing with or confronting someone,
- when someone asks something of you and saying "no" politely is a challenge,
- when you're asking for help you need from others, and
- when you're standing up for yourself because you feel you've been unfairly treated or someone has placed unreasonable expectations on you.

**Disagreeing or confronting**

Sometimes it can be intimidating to have to disagree with or confront someone. Many people feel uncomfortable about conflict. However, in these situations, it's important to be assertive so that the other person listens to you, understands you, and takes what you're saying into account.

**Saying "no"**

If someone asks for your help at work, it can be very difficult to say "no." You may fear causing offense or be intimidated by someone who orders you to do something. But it's crucial to be able to say "no" when appropriate in the workplace or your own performance may suffer.

**Asking for help**

It can be difficult to ask for help if you're struggling with a task or to complete your work on time. You may feel embarrassed or fear being thought of as inefficient. However, being assertive and honest is the best way to get the help you need.

### Standing up for yourself

If you feel that a rule is unfair or that you're being treated unfairly, it can be difficult to come forward to say how you feel – especially if nobody else says anything. But it's important that you assert your rights and be open about how you feel. This is often the only way to resolve the situation.

In this book, you'll learn why it's important to behave assertively and what this involves. You'll also learn how to be assertive yourself, even in difficult situations, while retaining good relationships with others. Ultimately, this will improve your interpersonal communication skills and enhance your effectiveness.

Suppose two new clothing stores have just opened in your area. One has its entrance down an alley, with a narrow front and closed doors leading down a flight of stairs. The other shop has an open front that you can walk into from the street. It has clothes on display outside and posters advertising new stock for the season. Which shop would you choose to visit?

Just as a place can look open and inviting, so too can another person. Some people are simply easier to get to know. Even when you meet them for the first time, they seem friendly and open. They are comfortable to be around and pleasant to interact with. In short, some people are more approachable than others.

If you're approachable, it means that others feel comfortable initiating conversations with you and talking with you. They are not treading on eggshells, worrying that they might be imposing on you, boring you, wasting your time, or offending you. Being approachable helps put shy people at ease. It breaks down barriers between people, enhancing communication and the flow of important information.

Being approachable can provide enormous value to you and to your organization. It can open the door to opportunities and help prevent problems. Being approachable generates rapport and motivates people. In these ways, approachability increases the chances of success in the workplace.

Whatever your basic personality, you've probably experienced times in your life when you needed to reach out to others or set them at ease but were not sure how to go about it. Being approachable is a social skill that anyone can master. It involves many different aspects, and you can develop these through understanding and practice.

This course can help you become more approachable by learning about these issues:
- the importance of approachability,
- how to reach out to others,
- how to invite others in, and
- how to put others at ease and build rapport.

As you develop your approachability, your ability to connect with people can enrich your life. It can improve your effectiveness at work and in social contexts.

# CHAPTER 1 - COMMUNICATING WITH CONFIDENCE

**CHAPTER 1 - Communicating with Confidence**
   SECTION 1 - Advantages and Elements of Confident Communication
   SECTION 2 - Trust, Credibility, and Communicating Confidently
   SECTION 3 - Confident Communication Behavior

# SECTION 1 - ADVANTAGES AND ELEMENTS OF CONFIDENT COMMUNICATION

**SECTION 1 - Advantages and Elements of Confident Communication**

Lack of confidence when communicating is a stressful problem, which can make it difficult for you to interact effectively with others. Although lack of confidence can manifest itself in a variety of ways, it is usually caused by a feeling of fear.

Anyone can become confident with practice once they understand how confidence is built. The key to building confidence is to earn the trust of others, establish your credibility, and carry yourself in a confident way. If you achieve these three goals, you can become a confident communicator.

# BENEFITS OF CONFIDENCE

**Benefits of confidence**

Most people have heard a saying similar to "with enough confidence, you can get almost anywhere you want to go." But what a lot of people don't know is that anyone can be confident with practice and an understanding of how confidence is built. Communicating well is a way to build your own confidence and the confidence of others in you.

Being confident gives you the ability to speak freely, without fearing what others may think of you. It enables you to be assertive, and it reduces anxiety in others. When you are confident, you listen better, because your perception of what others are saying is not distorted by fears and anxiety.

**Effects of low confidence on communication**

When you lack confidence, communicating is often associated with unpleasant emotions such as fear, anxiety, or anger. You may have distorted perceptions of what others think of you and what you are saying. You may feel that listeners are criticizing or judging you. You may even feel rejected, inadequate, frustrated, or resentful.

Lack of confidence can leave you feeling vulnerable, trapped, or isolated. This can make you hypersensitive, so you're easily hurt or upset. As a result, you may be quick to lose your temper or be unable to tolerate criticism. People who lack confidence often battle to express themselves, so communicating is exhausting and stressful.

When speakers lack confidence, listening to them can provoke negative feelings and impressions. You may also find that you react to a person who lacks confidence rather than to the message this person is conveying.

During interactions with speakers who lack confidence, it's harder to focus on the information being communicated and the interactions themselves are less satisfying. You may be less inclined to give speakers what they want, and they are less likely to help you or your organization to succeed.

Now that you have thought about some of the negatives, follow along as a confident communicator, Amrit, speaks to a colleague. Amrit needs Mario, the stock controller, to provide her with reports earlier than he has been so that she can determine what stock to purchase in good time.

**Amrit:** Hi, Mario. Thanks for the report yesterday. I can always rely on your reports to be accurate. But I'm worrying that the Paint Department is often under-stocked. What do you think?

*Amrit speaks clearly and audibly. She stands with her arms loosely at her side and maintains good eye contact.*

**Mario:** Yes, you're right. The stock always seems to arrive late. Why can't you keep our orders coming in fast enough?

**Amrit:** Well, it takes me a whole a day to source stock and get the paperwork in order. So the earlier I can get the reports, the quicker I can get the purchases in. Would it be possible for you to get them to me a day earlier?

*Amrit speaks clearly and audibly. Her tone is friendly and confident.*

**Mario:** Oh, I didn't realize it took so long on your side. I'll try to get the reports to you earlier.

**Amrit:** So I can expect the next report on Tuesday morning? Or would it suit you better to get it to me by close of business on Monday?

**Mario:** Actually, Monday would be better. Part of the problem is that mornings are very busy for me, so I often have distractions and other things to deal with. Giving you the report in the afternoon sounds like a much better idea.

There are several advantages to communicating confidently. Select each benefit of confident communication to learn more about it.

### More focused on what's being communicated

When you are confident, you can focus on the message itself and on understanding its meaning accurately, without distortions caused by insecurities. Your focus on what is communicated is also more likely to be mirrored by your listeners, because they won't be distracted by insecure communication behaviors on your part. If you're not worrying about how you come across, your listeners are less likely to focus on you and will listen to what you have to say.

### More satisfying

When you're speaking with confidence, both you and your listeners will be more relaxed and attentive. There is more harmonious communication, building a sense of cooperation toward a shared goal. Ultimately, goodwill is generated, and you and your listeners feel more satisfied.

### More likely to get what you want

When you are confident, people are more inclined to respond to you positively. Your confidence enables others to feel comfortable too. This means that they pay attention to what you are saying, so your message is clearer and has more influence over your listeners. This results in more favorable responses to your suggestions.

### Contributes to the success of your organization

Being confident results in fewer misunderstandings when communicating with colleagues, customers, and other parties. This preempts many problems and can significantly increase the efficiency and effectiveness of your organization. Additionally, being confident can give you more influence over customers or suppliers, who'll sense a cooperative attitude. They are then more likely to want to continue doing business with your organization.

### Question

What are some of the advantages of communicating with confidence?

Options:

1. You and the recipient will be more focused on what's being communicated
2. You and the recipient will find the exchange more satisfying
3. You'll be more likely to get what you want
4. You'll contribute to the success of your organization

## Interpersonal Communication

5. You'll be able to dominate in conversations
6. You'll avoid awkward situations

**Answer:**

Option 1: This option is correct. Communicating confidently enables both you and your listener to focus on what you're saying, rather than being distracted by negative internal emotions.

Option 2: This option is correct. Communicating with confidence reduces the stress levels for both you – as the speaker – and your listener. So you both gain greater satisfaction and enjoyment from your interaction.

Option 3: This option is correct. Confidence is essential for effective communication. When you speak confidently, you're far more likely to elicit a positive response to your suggestions or requests.

Option 4: This option is correct. Confidence enables good communication in most contexts, and good communication ensures things get done more effectively and efficiently in an organization.

Option 5: This option is incorrect. People who tend to dominate in conversations often suffer from poor confidence. And failing to listen can lead to damaging breakdowns in communication.

Option 6: This option is incorrect. Being confident doesn't prevent awkward situations from occurring. However, you may be able to deal with these situations with more grace when you're confident.

# ELEMENTS OF CONFIDENT COMMUNICATION

**Elements of confident communication**

Poor confidence can come across to others in many ways. For example, a person who isn't confident may seem submissive. Another person who lacks confidence may appear aggressive or domineering. In whatever way poor confidence manifests, the root cause is usually fear. A speaker who lacks confidence is most likely afraid.

There are many situational and personal factors that affect the level of confidence you have when communicating. These vary from situation to situation and person to person. For example, you may not feel confident because you are new to your position and are not experienced in working with customers.

Among the main factors that affect confidence in most communication environments are how listeners feel about the speaker, the communication history of the speaker, and the speaker's behavior during the communication – including how the speaker carries him or herself.

**Key elements of confident communication**

## Interpersonal Communication

It may seem that there are many key elements to communicating confidently, and individuals may find different elements useful for developing confidence in different situations.

However, these elements can generally be narrowed down to three that are essential. These include trust, credibility, and confident behavior when communicating.

Experts in communication have identified the following key elements as enabling confident communication: trust, credibility, and confident behavior when communicating.

**Trust**

Trust can be defined as the feeling you have that another person has good intentions and shares information openly and honestly. For you to trust another person, he or she has to be open to feedback and be able to admit to shortcomings. If you are open to feedback from others, for example, it enables trust because people feel safer when their views are taken into account. And when you know yourself to be trusted, you feel more confident.

**Credibility**

Credibility can be defined as being convincing or believable to others. Listeners decide whether a speaker is credible based on assessments of the speaker's motives, knowledge, and truthfulness. If you consistently keep your promises and honor your commitments, for instance, others find you credible. They can be sure that you keep your word. When others believe in what you say, you develop more confidence. Additionally, if you are accurate in what you say, this adds to your credibility.

**Confident behavior**

Confident behavior consists of the actions and mannerisms associated with confident communication. Open and relaxed body language, good posture, appropriate eye contact, and clear speaking are all examples of confident behavior. Others feel more comfortable around you when you behave confidently, and behaving in this way actually fosters a genuine feeling of confidence on your part.

Trust and credibility are closely related concepts, but they are not identical. Trust resides with the recipient, whereas credibility belongs to the speaker – in other words, I trust you because you are credible to me. Credibility is more rational, objective, and fact-based. Trust is more inherent and subjective.

For example, you may trust the bookkeeper in your organization for subjective reasons. However, her credibility will be based on her training and work experience, and her history of honest and accurate communication. To create confident communication, you need all three elements in place. If one is missing, your confidence will be eroded and information will not be effectively communicated.

If you lack the trust of your listeners or credibility among them, you cannot communicate with them effectively just by behaving – or trying to behave – confidently. Additionally, it's not possible to achieve credibility in an environment of mistrust, or vice versa.

**Question**

Which characteristics demonstrate the essential elements for confidence when communicating?

**Options:**

1. Being open to feedback from others

## Interpersonal Communication

2. Making only commitments that you can fulfill

3. Making appropriate eye contact with people you are communicating with

4. Sharing only accurate, factual information rather than theories or assumptions

5. Making only statements that you know other people agree with

**Answer:**

Option 1: This option is correct. When you're open to feedback, others will be able to trust you because they'll know their opinions will be considered. Trust is one of the essential elements required for effective and confident communication.

Option 2: This option is correct. If you speak and act with integrity, your words will be regarded as credible – and credibility is one of the essential elements for confident communication.

Option 3: This option is correct. Making eye contact is an important aspect of confident behavior.

Option 4: This option is incorrect. Sharing hypotheses and suppositions can bring valuable insights – provided you make it clear that you're not certain of the accuracy of your information.

Option 5: This option is incorrect. If you say only what you already know others agree with, people will realize that your statements aren't being made with the purpose of contributing new information. So they'll trust you less, and regard you as less credible.

# SECTION 2 - TRUST, CREDIBILITY, AND COMMUNICATING CONFIDENTLY

**SECTION 2 - Trust, Credibility, and Communicating Confidently**

The basic building block for confident communication is trust. You foster trust through specific behaviors such as being candid, admitting your errors, respecting others, and disclosing information freely. These trust-building behaviors contribute to your credibility as a communicator. Other factors that bolster credibility are your background, knowledge, and how you project competence when you communicate.

By improving trust and credibility, you generate rapport between yourself and your audience. This process is ongoing, interdependent, and fragile, so you need to be consistent. As rapport grows, you will gain confidence in yourself. Your audience will also gain confidence in you and will be more confident when talking to you.

# TRUST

**Trust**

Have you ever been in an environment where people were afraid to tell the truth? Where you weren't sure how much information you could share? Where you weren't sure who to trust? Or who trusted you? Without trust as a cornerstone, communicating is difficult. With trust, confident communication is much easier.

If you can build trust in interpersonal communication, each person is able to express themselves more confidently. If there is no trust, people become suspicious and aren't sure what they can say and what the consequences may be. This concept of trust is reciprocal. All communicating parties must trust one another for interpersonal communication to really work. This means you need to try to trust others to enable them to trust you too.

This trust is not instantaneous. It develops step by step, over time. Trust takes work; it needs to be practiced and earned before a low-trust environment can turn into a high-trust environment.

**Low-trust environment**

People in low-trust environments are suspicious of others' motives. When interpreting why others behave they way they do, people tend to assume the worst. This generally leads to more misunderstandings, low morale, and poor relationships.

**High-trust environment**

In higher-trust work environments, people tend to assume that others' motivations are positive. They are more open to giving people the "benefit of the doubt." This leads to a greater willingness to try to understand one another, improved morale, and more satisfying relationships.

It's clearly more beneficial and more comfortable to live and work in a high-trust environment. So building communication trust is important. To build this trust over time, you need to apply the following behavior:

- communicate productively,
- freely share information,
- be candid and truthful,
- accept constructive criticism, and
- respect other parties' needs and interests.

**Communicate productively**

Communicating productively means communicating with the aim of some positive or constructive outcome. Gossiping about someone's poor performance to a colleague doesn't meet these criteria. However, directly approaching a person and letting him know what he's doing right and how he might improve is productive. By giving constructive feedback or criticism, you help someone improve. When speaking with respect, you demonstrate that you value your relationship with the other party and further develop trust.

**Freely share information**

Freely sharing information means sharing all relevant information with people who need to know it. It's primarily about being forthcoming with information that others need. This also includes giving feedback and letting people know where they stand.

**It doesn't include breaking confidentiality**

When you share information, people feel trusted and trustworthy. They know what to do and why they need to do it. When you withhold information, people notice. This can result in anxiety, misunderstandings, wild speculation, and a drop in trust and productivity.

**Be candid and truthful**

When you are truthful, you don't exaggerate, omit, or spin the truth. This truthfulness provides the basis for trust. Others often know when they are not getting the full truth and interpret this as a betrayal. When you know the truth, you make better decisions, and do more. The same applies to those you communicate with. By being candid and truthful, you show your respect for those you are communicating with and demonstrate that you trust them with the information.

**Accept constructive criticism**

Learning from your mistakes is one of the quickest ways to grow and improve. By accepting constructive criticism, you show that you believe the person providing the feedback is interested in your well-being. If people know that you can accept constructive criticism gracefully, they won't be afraid of being truthful with you. Admitting it when you're wrong ensures you don't waste energy on covering up mistakes. Also, innovation requires risk taking and this can lead to mistakes. Without an environment supportive of learning from mistakes, innovation is lost.

**Respect others' needs and interests**

Being a trustworthy communicator involves respecting others, finding ways to speak to the other person's needs and interests, and honoring confidentiality. Breaches in confidentiality may cost you your job or a relationship. When information is sensitive or confidential, it's helpful to say you aren't able to share all the information. In this way, people feel informed, and that they can trust you with confidential information themselves. Respect for others and yourself fosters trust and also helps you become more confident and less self-critical.

Sally has been recruited as a line manager at a clothing manufacturer. Her supervisor, Scott, is orienting her to her work. Follow along as Scott tries to develop a trusting environment for interpersonal communication.

**Scott:** Hi, Sally. I know that we have put a lot on your plate without giving you time to settle in. I'm sorry about that. I'm here to find out how things are going so far. Do you need help with anything?

**Sally:** I'm really loving the hectic pace. I thrive on it really. However, I did miss the orientation meeting with the evening shift workers.

**Scott:** I like your enthusiasm. If you could combine that with careful planning, I think you'll get more results. I find a to-do list and reminders set on my PC really help me when things are new or overwhelming.

**Sally:** Thanks. I'll try that. I'm also wondering – is there some priority list or another way to organize all the information to get a bigger picture of what's going on?

**Scott:** You can use the weekly report template for a view of each area that needs attention and how they all fit together. The way it's structured really gives a good overview of what you need to be doing.

**Sally:** Great. I'll start there. And speaking of reports, I heard that the quarterly production rates and sales figures were pretty low. Is that true? And will it affect what we need to do?

**Scott:** I don't know the current figures yet, but as soon as I have them, I'll give the entire staff a briefing on how this will affect us. I should be receiving them tomorrow morning, and we can strategize then. Your division is generally our best performer, so I don't think you will be affected.

Scott began the conversation by admitting his and the company's mistakes – giving Sally a heavy workload before she had time to settle in. He then explored her needs and interests by asking her what she needed. He communicated productively by giving Sally advice. And he committed to share important information freely once he had it.

### Accepting constructive criticism

Suppose a manager tells her team that they should come to her with any complaints and can share their issues confidentially. However, if she then reprimands anyone who complains about anything, she has failed to create a trusting environment.

### Being candid and truthful

Many people avoid being candid and truthful, particularly when work environments change. For example, managers might say "current losses mean that the company will be cutting costs" – rather than something more truthful, such as "the company will be laying off approximately ten salespeople, and the choice will be based on average performance." Avoiding the truth in this situation opens the door to rumor, further anxiety, and mistrust.

**Question**

Donna is a third-party auditor who has been brought in to audit processes at a factory.

Which actions will help Donna foster trust among the factory's employees?

**Options:**

1. Explaining what her goals are, whose interests she represents, and why she is conducting her audit

2. Acknowledging the factory employees' busy schedules and avoiding disrupting their work without good cause

3. Communicating with employees only for the purpose of gaining an understanding of the factory processes

4. Accepting corrections from the employees regarding her understanding of the factory processes

5. Sharing audit information to help employees correct their mistakes before auditing the activities they're involved in

6. Freely sharing faults in the processes with the employees concerned and recording this information

**Answer:**

Option 1: This option is correct. By being candid about her goals and agenda, Donna will ensure that the employees are fully informed. This will foster their trust in her.

Option 2: This option is correct. Respecting the needs and interests of the employees will develop their trust in Donna.

Option 3: This option is incorrect. If Donna focuses exclusively on the task at hand, she will neglect other people's interests.

Option 4: This option is correct. Accepting constructive criticism is important for fostering trust. It's a way to show people that it is safe to offer their feedback, and that this feedback is valued.

Option 5: This option is incorrect. By enabling employees to correct mistakes before she audits them, Donna would be concealing faults in the factory processes. This violates the ethics of her profession, and therefore damages her trustworthiness

Option 6: This option is correct. Freely sharing information about faults in the processes enables employees to better understand and trust Donna's motives, as well as the insights she has to offer.

# CREDIBILITY

**Credibility**
Communicating in a way that builds trust increases your credibility as a communicator and your rapport with others. Credibility depends to a great extent on trust. And trust is dependent on credibility. If you have credibility, what you say is believable and people trust it. If people don't trust you, they won't believe you and you will lose credibility.

Trust-building behaviors create credibility over time, but this credibility is fragile and can be undermined or destroyed by just a few actions or words. First, admitting it when you're wrong enhances your sincerity in others' eyes and so builds your credibility. Not admitting your mistakes undermines both credibility and trust. Second, a reputation for exaggeration undermines people's belief in your honesty and candor. These behaviors can ruin your credibility.

From these examples, it's clear that trust earns and protects your credibility. But what other building blocks for credibility exist? Other important factors that help you to build credibility are your background and your use of behaviors that project credibility.

**Background**

There is a direct connection between credibility and your background, previous positions, successes, or accumulated expertise. Your background shapes people's perceptions of you. If you have experience or a prestigious position, others are more likely to see you as competent and credible.

**Behaviors**

Extrinsic behaviors can project competence and increase your credibility. They help you to project the image of a person who knows what he or she is talking about. This aspect of building credibility comes from your knowledge of the subject matter, use of confident body language, and the tone of voice that you use to deliver your message. You should also state clearly what you mean, keep your promises, and avoid using jargon.

Follow along as Sally discusses her progress in her new job. Try to notice where she is doing a good job of building credibility and where she is not.

I've been in the industry for five years. As a result of the more efficient processes I've identified here, I'm pleased to say that there has already been a reported 5% increase in the organization's productivity.

I believe that this increase will continue to grow exponentially! In terms of reporting, I've updated the TBS form and the WSR form, which now have a much higher validity-use ratio.

I have also been spending time getting to know my team members to gain a better perspective on who they are.

Sally's experience and enthusiasm are good credibility builders. Her body language is open and projects confidence. She begins the conversation well by establishing her background and giving a clear and unexaggerated account of the increase in productivity.

However, Sally then exaggerates the expected rate of improvement and begins to use jargon associated with reporting. These factors start to erode her credibility, and you may find that you are taking her less seriously by the time she begins speaking about her team.

So to build credibility, your behavior should foster trust and project confidence. These factors constantly interact to either increase or decrease your own and your audience's confidence in you. Increasing your credibility increases your confidence when communicating because you know others will have faith in what you are communicating.

**Question**

Max led an environmental research team investigating pollution and possible contamination of water tables in the area. Previous research efforts failed to produce useful results and his own team's results were delayed. He has been asked to present his findings to a group of stakeholders.

What should Max do to enhance his credibility during the presentation?

**Options:**

1. Research the subject, taking care not to get caught up in technical jargon
2. Admit the mistakes that occurred during the previous research and explain what he learned from them

3. Focus on areas he knows will interest his audience, like methods to ensure the water table remains pollution-free

4. Ignore any criticisms leveled at him and his team for the delay in getting the needed results

5. Name all pollution suspects, although the team is not yet sure who these may be

6. Ensure that his full credentials are mentioned when he is introduced to the group

**Answer:**

Option 1: This option is correct. If Max's presentation is well-researched, he will be more credible because he'll be able to demonstrate his knowledge of the subject.

Option 2: This option is correct. Not only is admitting mistakes a way for Max to be candid and open with his audience, but explaining what he learned from them is a way of sharing valuable information. Both of these trust-building behaviors will enhance his credibility.

Option 3: This option is correct. By focusing on the desired outcomes for the research team, he speaks to the interests of his audience and communicates productively. This builds trust, and therefore credibility.

Option 4: This option is incorrect. By ignoring constructive criticism, Max will reduce the trust of his audience. As well as showing that he's not open to sharing information, ignoring the criticisms may make it appear that Max is trying to cover up his mistakes. This will reduce trust, lowering Max's credibility.

Option 5: This option is incorrect. Doing this would be irresponsible and would show lack of respect for the named companies. This information is purely speculative, and providing it without evidence would lower Max's credibility.

Option 6: This option is correct. The group will take Max's background, qualifications, and previous experience into account when assessing his credibility as a speaker.

x

# RAPPORT AND CONFIDENCE

**Rapport and confidence**

The more your audience trusts you and believes in your credibility, the more you will feel confident when communicating. Increasing your trust and credibility strengthens your rapport with people.

When discussing communication, the term "rapport" has two distinct meanings. One is colloquial and the other technical. In this course, we use the colloquial definition, in which rapport refers to a meaningful and harmonious relationship.

Through strengthening rapport in your relationships, you are better able to communicate confidently and influence others. By building trust, credibility, and rapport, you also help others to communicate confidently with you. So everyone in the relationship benefits.

**Question**

How do trust and credibility help increase confidence in interpersonal communication?

**Options:**

1. By improving trust and credibility, you generate rapport with your audience, and this helps to build confidence

2. By behaving in ways that foster trust, you protect your credibility – if trust is lost, your credibility is lost too

3. By building trust and credibility, you feel more trustworthy and competent, which improves your confidence

4. By building trust and credibility, you help others to communicate confidently with you

5. By building trust, you're better able to ensure people do things your way and receive less opposition to your plans

6. By focusing on nurturing your credibility, you risk becoming arrogant rather than confident

**Answer:**

Option 1: This option is correct. Rapport is developed through the establishment of trust and credibility, and rapport helps to build confidence.

Option 2: This option is correct. If you are not trusted, what you say is unlikely to be seen as credible. Option 3: This option is correct. When you are regarded as trustworthy and credible, you build rapport with others, and this develops mutual confidence.

Option 4: This option is correct. Being trusted means that others feel safe communicating with you. In addition, trust and credibility build rapport. This gives others more confidence about communicating.

Option 5: This option is incorrect. Being trusted may allow you to communicate your ideas to people more effectively, and it gives your ideas some credibility. Being trusted does not enable you to impose your ideas on others.

Option 6: This option is incorrect. Credibility is earned from others. You cannot develop much credibility while being arrogant, because arrogance causes people to lose trust in your motives and opinions.

# SECTION 3 - CONFIDENT COMMUNICATION BEHAVIOR

**SECTION 3 - Confident Communication Behavior**

When preparing to communicate, you need to ensure that your appearance projects the image that you want it to. You should be clear about what you want to say, why you want to say it, and who your audience is. You should also prevent negative self-talk and ease your anxiety by ensuring you're prepared for the worst possible outcome, so you know you'll be able to handle this.

To use your voice confidently, take note of how you use inflections, tone, volume, and speed. Confident body language includes alert and relaxed posture, and good eye contact. You should use spontaneous and open gestures to add meaning to your message, and ensure your facial expressions match the content of your message.

# PREPARING FOR CONFIDENT COMMUNICATION

**Preparing for confident communication**
When a seasoned communicator "wows" a crowd, it often seems effortless. However, speaking with confidence takes preparation and practice. When preparing to communicate, it's helpful to develop the personal image you want to project. You need to know what you want to say and how you can address your fears and any negative self-talk.

**Develop your personal image**
Being comfortable in your clothing and dressing appropriately for the occasion help you to feel more confident. When you look good – for example, wearing colors and styles that suit you – you feel more confident. If you're not certain what looks best, ask friends or professionals to help you. Typically, your style should aim to express who you are without making you either stand out or blend in too much. So you need some measure of self-awareness – you need to be aware of how you look,

and then you can design the image that you want to project.

**Know what you want to say**

Knowing what you want to say in advance helps you to feel prepared and competent. So you need to prepare your message ahead of time if you think you might have trouble conveying it. Consider where your message may be unclear, because people don't always ask questions. Ensure the message is simple and specific, and includes arguments or examples to support your main points.

Also try to keep in mind who your audience is. Knowing what they want and what their interests are can help you to speak to those interests while conveying your message. Another important part of what you want to say is why you want to say it. If you have a clear purpose, your message itself becomes clearer and you have a better understanding of what you want to say.

**Address fears and self-talk**

You may find that you are worrying when speaking, telling yourself that you will make mistakes or be rejected by your listeners. This type of self-talk erodes your confidence and increases stress. You can address these fears by consciously speaking to yourself as you would to a good friend – encourage and bolster yourself. Live in the present and soothe yourself so that you don't worry. Another useful strategy is to imagine the worst possible outcome, and prepare yourself for it. If you are prepared, you are even more likely to succeed.

When considering the image you want to project, remember that different clothes may be suitable for different situations. Boardroom meetings usually require one style of dressing, whereas team-building outings require another. To help you determine what you want to say, you can ask yourself the following questions: Why do I want to say this? What about this communication would interest my listener? How clear is my argument? And have I provided examples or evidence to support my main ideas?

Once you know what you want to say, consider preparing for the worst. Suppose you want a colleague to inform you as soon as a story is ready for editing. The worst outcome may be the colleague ignoring your request and saying that it's not his responsibility. You can now plan for that contingency so that you'll know how to respond.

Finally, be kind to yourself. If someone you cared about was anxious, you would soothe them rather than attack them with negativity. The same should hold true in the way you treat yourself.

**Question**

Which techniques will help you prepare for confident communication?

**Options:**

1. Creating the personal image you want to project
2. Being clear on what you want to communicate
3. Addressing your fears and changing negative self-talk to positive self-talk
4. Not letting yourself think about what could possibly go wrong
5. Dressing the same way that people you admire dress

**Answer:**

Option 1: This option is correct. By being aware of the image you want to project, being comfortable with that image, and knowing what you are projecting, you can bolster your confidence.

Option 2: This is a correct option. Knowing what you want to say and why you want to say it helps to reduce anxiety. By carefully preparing the content of your message, you increase your confidence in relaying that message.

Option 3: This option is correct. By being kind to yourself, preparing for the worst, and living in the moment, rather than worrying about the communication to come, you increase your confidence.

Option 4: This option is incorrect. If you're feeling anxious, it's useful to imagine the worst possible outcome and to prepare for that. This increases your confidence that you can handle the communication.

Option 5: This option is incorrect. Your style should reflect who you are, and you should be comfortable with that style.

# CONFIDENT VOCALIZATION

**Confident vocalization**

As you know, it can be uncomfortable to listen to someone who shouts, whispers, mumbles, or drones on in a monotone. Using your voice with confidence makes your and your audience's experience much more pleasurable.

**Inflection**

Your voice's inflection is how it rises and falls as you speak. Without inflection, you will speak in a monotone, which is boring for listeners to follow. If your inflection rises and falls too often, it creates a sing-song effect that is difficult to take seriously. When your inflection or pitch goes down at the end of a sentence, it shows certainty and is authoritative. When your inflection goes up at the end of a sentence, it indicates a question or uncertainty. Your inflection can also be used to show emotion – rising with anger, lowering with sadness, and so on.

**Volume**

A confident voice is audible but not overpowering. If you shout, your audience will back away from your message. If you speak very quietly, people will struggle to hear you and may become frustrated or disinterested. Speaking audibly engenders confidence in the speaker as well as conveying confidence to the listener. People are more likely to overrule what you say if they struggle to hear it, which can create a cycle of weakening confidence. If you know that your voice is too quiet, practice speaking more loudly and opening your mouth to accentuate each word.

**Tone**

Your tone of voice indicates when you are joking, serious, upset, angry, and so on. When speaking, you need to ensure that your tone matches what you want to say. If people think that you are joking when you are serious, you are not getting your message across. Typically, people find a lower tone more authoritative than a higher-pitched tone.

**Speed**

The speed at which you talk affects your confidence and the confidence your audience has in you. Confident speech is typically fluent and slow enough for people to follow with ease, and free of lengthy pauses. Speaking rapidly often indicates nervousness and makes it difficult for a listener to follow your message. This is especially problematic when speaking in groups, because people in group situations are less likely to ask you to slow down.

If you hesitate or pause frequently when you speak, your listeners will sense your uncertainty and may become bored waiting for your message to arrive. If you prepare well, you will hesitate less. If you aren't able to express yourself without hesitations in a particular situation, speak to those involved later – once you are clear on what you need to say.

Rosa, William, and Taku work at a software development company. They're in a meeting to discuss a project that's behind schedule. Follow along as they discuss the problem. Think about who conveys confidence and who doesn't. Pay particular attention to inflection, volume, tone, and speed.

**William:** At our current rate, we won't be able to complete the project on time. I think we'll need to bring another programmer on to the project. What do you both think? William speaks slowly without hesitation. His inflection goes down at the end of the first two sentences and goes up at the end of the final sentence. His tone is serious and he speaks clearly and audibly.

**Rosa:** I don't know – it may take too long to train someone. Perhaps if we put in a few extra hours we could get on top of the deadlines. Rosa speaks quickly, but audibly. Her inflection rises at the end of each sentence. Her tone is quite high-pitched and anxious.

**Taku:** Umm...I think, I think that the recent changes to scope are the real problem. The new stuff is complex and, umm, will simply take longer...perhaps we should ask the client if we can get an extension. Taku speaks slowly with several hesitations. His voice is quiet. His inflection goes up at the end of each sentence. His tone conveys that he is joking.

### Question

Think about the conversation between William, Rosa, and Taku. Who conveyed confidence?

### Options:

1. William

2. Rosa
3. Taku

**Answer:**

Option 1: This is the correct option. William speaks with confidence – he speaks fluently and without hesitation. His inflection goes down at the end of the first two sentences, conveying certainty. It then goes up at the end of the final sentence, to indicate a question. His tone is serious and he speaks clearly and audibly.

Option 2: This option is incorrect. Although Rosa speaks audibly, she speaks too quickly and her inflection rises at the end of each sentence, conveying lack of certainty. Her tone is also quite high-pitched and anxious.

Option 3: This is an incorrect option. Taku conveys anxiety and lack of confidence. He speaks slowly, with hesitation and several pauses, and this conveys uncertainty. His voice is quiet and difficult to hear. His inflection goes up at the end of each sentence, which also conveys uncertainty. Also, his tone suggests that he is joking, although what he has to say should be taken seriously.

In the example, William is the only one of the group who uses his voice with confidence. His inflection conveys certainty, except when he asks a question. He speaks fluently and at a pace that is easy to follow. His voice is loud enough to be heard without being dominating. Also, his tone is serious, which matches his message.

The volume of Rosa's voice is fine. However, she needs to speak slower and lower her inflection at the end of each sentence. Her tone also conveys anxiety, so if she can develop a calmer tone, she'll project more confidence.

Taku requires quite a bit of practice with his vocalization. He needs to increase the volume and pace of his voice. He should also avoid sounding as though he is joking when he is serious. In other words, his tone should match his message. His inflections convey a lack of certainty, so practicing lowering his inflection at the end of each sentence should help him project greater confidence.

**Case Study: Question 1 of 1**
**Scenario**

Amrit, Mario, and Tina work at a large hardware store. Follow their conversation as they discuss the planning for a team-building weekend for the staff.

**Amrit:** I looked into a venue for our team-building weekend, and I've found two that sound good. The first is a resort an hour's drive from here. It's next to a large lake, with little chalets in the woods next to the water.

Amrit speaks slowly without hesitation. Her inflection goes down at the end of each sentence. Her tone is enthusiastic and she speaks clearly and audibly.

**Mario:** We've got a limited amount to spend per head, so I need to see a quotation for the weekend for each venue. Last year we didn't come in under budget.

Mario speaks audibly, but quickly. He doesn't use inflection, so his voice is monotone. His tone is disinterested.

**Tina:** I've got some, umm, ideas for...team-building exercises. So far, we have...ahh...a number of possibilities. We need to organize workshops, and we also need to have fun, I think. Maybe boat races would be fun.

Tina speaks slowly with several hesitations. Her voice is quiet. Her inflection goes down at the end of each sentence. Her tone is calm and serious.

**Question**

Count the number of confident vocalization characteristics for each character. Then determine your answer based on who has the most characteristics that convey confidence.

Whose communication was the most confident based on vocalization characteristics?

**Options:**

1. Tina
2. Amrit
3. Mario

**Answer:**

Option 1: This option is incorrect. Tina's use of inflection shows certainty, but this is undermined by her quiet and hesitant speech. Her tone is calm and serious and so undermines the content of her message, which relates to having fun.

Option 2: This is the correct option. Amrit uses all of the characteristics of confident vocalization. She speaks at a moderate pace, without hesitation. Her inflection goes down at the end of each sentence, conveying certainty. Her tone is enthusiastic, which matches the content of her message, and she speaks clearly at a confident volume.

Option 3: This option is incorrect. The volume of Mario's voice is confident. However, because he doesn't use inflection, speaks too quickly, and has a disinterested tone, his communication lacks confidence.

# CONFIDENT BODY LANGUAGE

**Confident body language**

How you use your voice can affect your projection of confidence when communicating. So can how you use your body. Confident communication relies on your posture, eye contact, gestures, and facial expressions.

**Posture**

How you carry yourself tells your listeners something about you and about how you feel about your listeners. Standing tall with your hands loosely by your sides shows that you are alert and relaxed. If you are sitting, you should sit upright with your arms by your sides, resting either on the arm rests, the seat, or on your thighs. A posture that is alert and relaxed helps you to become more alert and relaxed, and conveys confidence in yourself and interest in your audience.

**Eye contact**

A steady gaze mixed with brief periods of looking away can be used to convey respect and interest in a person, and will enhance your message.

The most important guide to eye contact is the other person looking back at you. When talking with a person who avoids eye contact, it may help to glance periodically at the person to show that he or she has your attention, and then to look away to set the person at ease.

**Gestures and expressions**

Facial expressions and gestures are important ways of conveying information. If they don't match your words, you'll give mixed messages and appear inauthentic or unconvincing. So your face and your gestures should say the same thing that your words do. Facial expressions and body movements can give descriptive qualities and emphasis to what you are saying, and so add meaning. Smiling and using open, relaxed, spontaneous gestures convey a relaxed warmth and build confidence.

If your posture is rigid and tense, you communicate insecurity or anxiety. If you slouch, you convey a lack of interest in your audience. Avoiding eye contact can cause you to miss important responses from your listeners, distances you from them, and conveys a lack of self-confidence. But excessive eye contact – or staring – is considered rude. It makes others uncomfortable, and they may interpret it as aggression.

Although smiling is often a sign of confidence, smiles should not be forced or used in serious moments in a conversation. Overusing gestures is distracting, whereas if you don't move at all, you'll appear tense. It's important to find an appropriate balance.

**Case Study: Question 1 of 2**
**Scenario**

## Interpersonal Communication

Sally, the line manager at a clothing manufacturer, has asked her supervisor, Scott, for his advice on the best place to put their new T-shirt printing machine.

**Scott:** How about putting the printer close to the rack so we can hang the T-shirts immediately? Scott has good posture, and seems relaxed, yet alert. His expression doesn't change and he doesn't smile. He gestures with his hands as he speaks. Sally is listening, looking at Scott intently, and frowning slightly with concentration. Her arms are crossed.

**Scott:** Then there'll be no chance of smudging any wet prints by accident. Scott is not looking at Sally. His expression has not changed. Sally is looking at Scott. Her position has not changed much.

**Sally:** Yes, I think that's the right location, but we'll need to connect the printer to the computer, and it's on the other side of the factory. Sally is looking at Scott's face, with her head slightly bent, and a serious expression on her face. Her hands folded in front of her crossed. Scott is still looking away, and his face is not expressive.

**Sally:** We actually need to bring in a new computer to manage this machine, so if anything goes wrong, it can be sorted out at once on both ends. Maybe we should create a workstation between the machine and the rack. Sally follows Scott's gaze outward, and has a contemplative expression on her face. Her hands behind her back. Scott has not changed his position or expression much.

**Question**

What characteristics of Scott's body language showed confidence?

**Options:**

1. Scott makes good eye contact with Sally

2. Scott's posture conveys confidence
3. Scott gestures confidently
4. Scott's facial expressions convey confidence

**Answer:**

Option 1: This option is incorrect. Scott doesn't make enough eye contact with Sally. He fails to engage with her on this level and might miss some important facial expressions of hers.

Option 2: This option is correct. Scott stands well. He's not too rigid and upright, nor is he slouching. He has a poised, relaxed posture that gives the impression of confidence.

Option 3: This option is correct. Scott uses his hands openly and descriptively to add to the meaning of his words. This is appropriate during his conversation with Sally and conveys confidence.

Option 4: This option is incorrect. Scott's facial expression is too serious and unchanging. He misses valuable opportunities to respond to what Sally is saying, which may decrease rapport.

Case Study: Question 2 of 2

What characteristics of Sally's body language showed confidence?

**Options:**

1. Sally makes good eye contact with Scott
2. Sally's posture is confident
3. Sally has confident gestures
4. Sally's facial expressions convey confidence

**Answer:**

Option 1: This option is correct. Sally looks at Scott's eyes and face often, but she doesn't hold her gaze when it's not reciprocated. She modifies her eye contact to suit Scott's responses.

Option 2: This option is not correct. Sally's tense posture conveys anxiety rather than confidence.

Option 3: This option is incorrect. Sally doesn't convey confidence with her gestures. She keeps her arms closed, or behind her, and doesn't use gestures to describe or emphasize what she's saying.

Option 4: This option is correct. Sally uses her facial expressions to augment what she's saying and to convey her feelings and thoughts.

It's important to stay in touch with your thoughts and feelings while you are communicating. Worrying or criticizing yourself reduces your confidence and your ability to communicate.

When you notice negative thoughts, replace them with positive and encouraging thoughts. Encouraging thoughts support you in your task and give you the confidence you need to succeed.

You need to focus on the present to avoid worrying. When you set your worries aside and think about what you are doing now, your mind can concentrate on your present task. Your anxiety is reduced, so you become more confident and effective.

It's helpful to pay attention to how your body feels. If your heartbeat is high, your stomach is queasy, or you feel tension in your muscles, you are probably feeling anxious. By focusing on your breathing and consciously relaxing your muscles, you can calm yourself.

**Case Study: Question 1 of 2**
**Scenario**

Sorin Dumitrascu

Sally is preparing to inform her team that they won't be receiving a bonus this quarter due to low profits. She is very nervous about giving the group this news, so she has asked you to assess her speech. Follow along as she gives the speech.

Hi everyone. I've called this meeting to...um...clarify what has been happening this quarter with the company...and...how this will impact you. Sally is standing tall with one hand loosely by her side and the other palm out toward you. She is looking directly at the you. She speaks clearly but hesitantly with a calm and serious tone. She lowers the inflection of her voice at the end of her sentences.

As you already know, your performance this quarter has been the best of all our teams, and...I...ah...really want to thank you for all the effort you've put in. Sally is smiling with both hands held loosely by her sides. She is looking directly at you. She speaks clearly but hesitantly with a sad tone. She lowers the inflection of her voice at the end of the sentence.

However, the company's profits this quarter are down 25%...which...is a really big margin for us – the biggest drop in five years. Sally is standing tall and looking down slightly. She speaks clearly but hesitantly with a cheerful tone. She emphasizes the word "really" and lowers the inflection of her voice at the end of her sentences.

Our analysts believe that this trend won't continue into the next quarter, so...ah...there's no need to worry about any long-term fallout from this. Sally is standing tall and is looking directly at you. She speaks clearly but hesitantly, with a calm and serious tone. She lowers the inflection of her voice at the end of her sentences.

But... um... in the short term, this is going to...ah...impact us. The company can't...ah...provide us...with bonuses...for this quarter. Sally is standing tall, with one hand extended and the other on her chin. She is smiling nervously. She speaks clearly but hesitantly with a very nervous tone. She lowers the inflection of her voice at the end of her sentences.

I'm... really sorry. I know many of you were counting on getting the bonus. But...um...indicators suggest that next quarter, bonuses will be reinstated. Are there any questions? Sally is standing tall with one hand loosely by her side and the other palm out toward you. She is looking directly at you. She speaks clearly but hesitantly with a calm tone. She emphasizes the word "sorry" and lowers the inflection of her voice at the end of her sentences. For the question, she raises her inflection at the end of the sentence.

**Question**

What statements about the effectiveness of Sally's communication are true?

**Options:**

1. The way she delivered her speech conveys authoritative certainty about her message

2. Her smile when she spoke about the team's excellent performance makes her statement seem more authentic

3. Smiling as she tells the team about the lack of a bonus softens the blow for the team

4. Standing tall with her hands loosely at her sides conveys that she is not interested in what she is saying

5. Sally conveys respect and interest by maintaining good eye contact

**Answer:**

Option 1: This option is incorrect. Sally's speech was delivered in a halting, hesitating manner that overshadowed several of the things she did manage to do well. Her inflection, which normally would've been fine, was hard to follow as it was broken up by the hesitation of her speech. Overall, she didn't convey authoritative certainty.

Option 2: This option is correct. By matching her facial expression to the content of her message, which involved praise for her team, Sally conveys authenticity.

Option 3: This option is incorrect. Sally should match her facial expressions to her message. If she looked upset as she told the team the news, she would project more authenticity.

Option 4: This is an incorrect option. Sally's posture conveys relaxed alertness, which is a positive, confident behavior.

Option 5: This option is correct. A steady gaze conveys respect and interest. Sally managed this well. Correct answer(s):

2. Her smile when she spoke about the team's excellent performance makes her statement seem more authentic

5. Sally conveys respect and interest by maintaining good eye contact

**Case Study: Question 2 of 2**

What confident communication behaviors does Sally need to improve?

**Options:**

1. She needs to work on projecting her voice so that it's fully audible

2. She needs to speak with less hesitation

3. She needs to ensure that her vocal tone matches the tone of her message

4. She needs to use gestures to enhance the meaning of her message

**Answer:**

Option 1: This option is incorrect. Sally spoke clearly and audibly throughout her communication.

Option 2: This option is correct. Sally hesitated often, which conveys lack of certainty and could result in her losing her audience's attention.

Option 3: This option is correct. Sally used inappropriate tones, often sounding light or overly cheerful when she was serious, and sounding sad when she was congratulating her team.

Option 4: This option is incorrect. Sally used appropriate gestures, which enhanced her message.

# CHAPTER 2 - TARGETING YOUR MESSAGE

**CHAPTER 2 - Targeting Your Message**
   SECTION 1 - <u>Essential Elements of Targeted Communications</u>
   SECTION 2 - <u>Planning Your Communication</u>
   SECTION 3 - <u>Delivering Your Message and Getting Feedback</u>

# SECTION 1 - ESSENTIAL ELEMENTS OF TARGETED COMMUNICATIONS

## SECTION 1 - Essential Elements of Targeted Communications

A basic communication model consists of five components – the sender and receiver, the medium, contextual factors, the message, and feedback. Because each component is affected by many variables and varies across situations, it's essential that communicators take the time and effort to plan and target their messages carefully.

# COMPONENTS OF COMMUNICATION

**Components of communication**

American composer John Powell once said, "Communication works for those who work at it." One of the ways to work at improving your communication skills is to understand the different components involved in all communication. A basic communication model consists of five components. These are the sender and receiver, the medium used to carry the message, contextual factors surrounding the message, the message itself, and feedback from the receiver.

To target your messages effectively, you need to consider the variables that can affect each of the components in the model. Communication can go awry if just one of these variables is out of sync. For example, even the best of messages won't get through properly if the intended receiver is surrounded by too much background noise to hear it properly.

Certain factors can complicate communication between a sender and receiver. These factors include people's different beliefs, values, and personalities, as well as various barriers to communication.

**Beliefs, values, and personalities**

People have different beliefs, values, and personalities, and these heavily influence the way they perceive information. So senders and receivers may have different reactions to the same information. This makes communication especially complex.

**Barriers to communication**

Various barriers can prevent a sender's message from being understood as intended. Examples include bad grammar and word choice, and the nature of the relationship between the sender and receiver. In an already strained relationship, for instance, poor choice of words could be disastrous because of the emotionally charged atmosphere between the sender and receiver. It's important to create and deliver messages in a way that overcomes these barriers.

The medium is the means by which a message is delivered. For example, you communicate through speech in a face-to-face conversation, as well as through e-mail, an instant message, a telephone call, or a written letter.

To choose the right medium, you should consider several factors. These include the importance of the message, practicality, your and the receiver's preferences, the receiver's communication style, and whether there's a need for feedback.

**Importance**

Generally, you should deliver really important messages face-to-face or over the phone. This makes more impact and enables the receiver to respond immediately. E-mail is suitable for less important messages, or those to which you don't need an urgent response. Instant messaging is best used for casual messages.

**Practicality**

When senders and receivers are geographically dispersed, using telecommunications media – such as the phone, e-mail, and instant messaging – is more practical than arranging face-to-face meetings. Also, it's more practical to use a text-based medium like e-mail if you need to send someone a lot of data or to keep a record of what's discussed. Other practical considerations are the costs, physical space requirements, and potential delays associated with using different communication media.

**Preferences**

Some people just prefer certain media over others. To communicate effectively, you should consider the other party's preference in this regard. Sometimes this may also be influenced by the established communication processes in the person's organization.

**Receiver's communication style**

Some people respond best to information that's presented visually. Others rely more on what they hear, or on information that's text-based. And some learn best by doing – building models or putting ideas into practice. In trying to choose an effective medium, you should consider the preferred communication style of the receiver. For example, a receiver with a predominantly visual style is likely to respond better to a diagram than to a detailed explanation of a process over the phone.

You should also consider the receiver's willingness to receive your message. For example, it's better to communicate sensitive information that might upset the receiver in person, rather than via e-mail or an instant message.

**Feedback**

If you need feedback from the receiver without delay, you should choose a medium that allows this – like a face-to-face meeting or a phone call. If the need for feedback is less urgent, a medium like e-mail might be appropriate. If you don't require feedback at all, you can opt for a less personal medium that doesn't support two-way communication. For example, you might use a poster.

Various contextual factors can play a role in how well a sender and receiver of a message communicate. Among these factors are body language, timing, and the environment – or setting – in which the message is delivered.

**Body language**

Body language refers to all the nonverbal ways people communicate, including facial expressions, physical gestures, and posture. In face-to-face conversations, these play an important role. They often communicate things that are left unsaid, such as a person's enthusiasm, attentiveness, or even annoyance.

When you're speaking to someone, it's important to ensure your body language is appropriate. It's also important to read the other person's body language so you can respond to it.

**Timing**

The timing of a message can influence how well or badly it's received. For example, if you won't make an important deadline, it's better to let your manager know well in advance, rather than announcing this at the last minute. It's also best to time messages for when you know the receiver has time to attend to them properly.

**Environment**

Factors like the formality or informality of a setting, noise in the surroundings, and room temperature can all affect the abilities of a sender and receiver to communicate. Their physical proximity also plays a role. For example, sitting close to another person encourages communication that's more emotional and personal.

You also need to consider these contextual factors when you communicate with others: the type of language you use for your message the assumptions you make when formulating your message the willingness of the receiver to engage in dialog about your message, and your tone of voice, volume, and the rate at which you speak

Communication can also be distorted by "noise." Noise can be defined as anything that causes a receiver to incorrectly receive the message the sender intends to communicate. Examples of noise include distracting sounds, faulty hearing, mispronunciation, and errors in transferring the message from sender to receiver.

For example, when an e-mail is partially cut off during data transmission, it has been distorted by the "noise" of a technical error. As a communicator, some noise factors are within your control, and some are not. A message is defined as the object of communication, or more simply, the thing that is being communicated.

A message may take a number of forms, including spoken, written, visual, and physical signals. Some qualities of a message include its wording, directness, and purpose. Each message has a specific purpose. For example, the purpose of a message can be to inform, persuade, inspire, stimulate, or entertain.

### Inform

A message may be designed to convey important facts or information. For example, you update your manager on progress in a particular project, or send staff detailed instructions on how to complete a task.

### Persuade

The purpose of a message can be to persuade the receiver to accept or reject certain conditions or actions. For instance, you deliver a proposal outlining the benefits of a new project to persuade managers to support the project.

### Inspire

A message can be designed to motivate the receiver to act in a specific way. For example, the leader of a sales team sends team members a motivational message in an attempt to inspire them to meet their quarterly sales targets.

### Stimulate

The purpose of a message can be to stimulate discussion about a particular issue. For instance, you send a friend a news article and ask for her opinion of the story.

### Entertain

A message can be designed to entertain the receiver. For example, you send a colleague who's struggling to compile a financial report a light-hearted e-mail that pokes fun at the tediousness of company budgets.

Messages can have many other purposes, like instructing, warning, greeting, or requesting information. For a message to be effective, you should know exactly why you plan to send it.

Feedback is any response to a communicated message. It takes the form of a message itself, and may be verbal, visual, or written. Often, feedback is essential, because it's what turns one-way communication into two-way communication. Feedback may be either positive or negative.

**Positive feedback**

Positive feedback indicates the receiver has received and understood the message.

**Negative feedback**

Negative feedback indicates that the receiver either has not received the message or has not understood its content.

Feedback is important during communication because it helps the sender to make any necessary adjustments so that the message is correctly received. Feedback is also important after you've delivered a message. It enables further clarification or discussion. It can also help the sender and receiver recognize what was or wasn't effective in the communication of the original message.

The sheer number of variables involved make communication a complex process. To navigate this process and communicate effectively, you need to target your messages to the intended receivers.

**Question**

Why do you think it's important to plan and target your messages carefully?

**Options:**

1. Each receiver may react differently to a particular message

2. Proper planning allows you to use the communication medium you're most comfortable with

3. Targeting your message guarantees that your receiver will understand it

4. Identifying the purpose of your message helps you to construct the message in a clearer way

**Answer:**

Option 1: The way receivers react to a message is heavily influenced by their beliefs, values, and personalities – all of which vary from person to person.

Option 2: The choice of medium should depend on the situation – not your personal preference. Several factors should influence your choice of communications media, including practicality, the importance of the message, and the receiver's preference.

Option 3: Event if you've targeted your message correctly, a number of factors, such as a poor choice of words or bad grammar, could act as noise – distorting the receiver's understanding of your message.

Option 4: Messages can have many purposes, like instructing, warning, greeting, or requesting information. If you're not sure why you're sending the message, it's likely that your receiver won't find the message to be clear.

When crafting a message for a particular purpose, it's essential to consider who the receiver is, which medium to use, what the contextual factors are, what the message itself is, and how you can attain positive feedback.

By taking the time to think through each aspect and to plan appropriately, you can improve your communication skills, ensuring that you deliver effective, targeted messages every time.

**Question**

Mario is too ill to go to work. He wants to inform his manager, Jim. Match each of the components of the communication model to an example of it in this situation.

**Options:**

A. Receiver
B. Medium
C. Contextual factor
D. Message
E. Feedback
F. Sender

**Targets:**

1. Jim
2. Telephone call
3. The time is 8:00 a.m.
4. "I'm really ill, so I'm afraid I won't be coming in to work today."
5. "Thanks for letting me know. Get well soon."
6. Mario

**Answer**

Jim, the manager, receives the message from Mario, his employee.

The telephone is an example of a communication medium – it's what Mario uses to transfer his message to his manager.

The timing of a message is an example of a contextual factor. In this example, 8:00 a.m. – the beginning of the work day – is an appropriate time for Mario to send his message.

The message itself is that Mario is ill and won't be able to make it to work.

Jim's feedback is positive – acknowledging that he has received and understood the message.

## Interpersonal Communication

In the example, Mario is the sender – the person who sends the original message – to inform his manager that he's ill and won't be coming in to work.

# SECTION 2 - PLANNING YOUR COMMUNICATION

**SECTION 2 - Planning Your Communication**

To create and deliver effective, targeted messages, you need to analyze the receiver, plan the context, plan and deliver your message, and then get feedback.

In analyzing the receiver, you consider the receiver's responsibilities and interests, knowledge level, and preferences. Planning the context for communicating a message involves choosing the most appropriate medium, timing, and setting for delivering the message. This will depend on the importance of the message and on the characteristics and preferences of the receiver.

# ANALYZING THE RECEIVER

**Analyzing the receiver**

To create and deliver targeted messages, you need to complete four steps. First analyze the receiver – the person to whom you want to deliver the message. Next, plan the context, and then plan and deliver your message. Finally, get feedback to ensure that your message has been understood.

Analyzing the intended receiver of your message is the first step because the information this gives you should inform the rest of the communication process. It involves considering the needs, wants, and priorities of the person you plan to address so that you can target your message effectively.

To analyze the intended receiver, you can ask yourself several questions:
- What are the receiver's responsibilities and interests?
- What is the receiver's current knowledge level?

- What preferences does the receiver have in terms of communication medium, context, and strategy?

People are more attentive to messages that clearly relate to them. So, in targeting a message, you should always consider the receiver's responsibilities and interests. For example, what are this person's work responsibilities? Also, does the receiver have any political interests you should bear in mind?

**Work responsibilities**

The relevance of your message will be clear to a receiver if it relates to the tasks this person has to complete at work. For example, if you're selling a computer program, you might focus on how the product can simplify your receiver's work tasks – rather than just listing the product's general capabilities.

**Political interests**

Your message may impact the political interests of the receiver – that is, the agenda that the receiver is trying to push in the organization. If your message risks venturing into this territory, you'll have to be careful to communicate in a way that advances your own purpose, rather than becoming too drawn into office politics or interpersonal conflict.

For example, your company is restructuring and a supervisor is jockeying for a higher-level position. You need to ask him to work overtime. Your request should mention the potential benefits of the overtime in terms of his ambition for a promotion.

If you personalize your communication for the receiver, you show that you're acknowledging her interests. In turn, this makes the receiver more likely to react positively to your message.

When considering the receiver's current level of knowledge, you should ask yourself three main questions: "What information does the receiver have?" "What information does the receiver require?" and "What jargon or work-related details is the receiver familiar with?"

John, the managing editor of a newspaper, is disappointed with a draft article that Todd submitted. Todd used to be the newspaper's IT technician, and is now trying his hand at writing. Follow along as John and Todd discuss problems with the article.

**John:** Todd, I'm afraid there are a lot of problems with your draft article on open-source technology. It seems to be incomplete.

*John is disappointed.*

**Todd:** I'm not sure what you mean. I used the sources you gave me and I think I covered all the major points in your brief.

*Todd is confused.*

**John:** Yes, but what about the basics? There's no infographic and no nutgraph. There aren't even any cutlines for your screenshots! And where are the pull quotes? In May, I sent all the journalists that report about how essential pull quotes are to a piece.

*John is upset.*

**Todd:** I only started writing for the company in July. Also, I don't think I understand what you're saying. I'll have to ask another writer to help me with this.

*Todd is frustrated*

In this case, John – Todd's manager – failed to analyze the receiver of his message. As a result, Todd was left frustrated and confused.

**Question**

Which basic questions has John failed to ask?
**Options:**
1. What information does the receiver have?
2. What information does the receiver require?
3. What jargon is the receiver familiar with?

**Answer:**

Option 1: This option is incorrect. Todd explained that he used the resources John had given him, so there was no need to ask what information Todd had.

Option 2: This is a correct option. This communication was ineffective because John assumed that Todd had the pull quotes report. So, he didn't ask whether Todd required the information.

Option 3: This option is correct. This communication was ineffective because John used jargon that Todd didn't understand.

To be effective, a message should contain exactly the information that the recipient requires from you, in a form that this person will be able to understand easily. You should also be careful to exclude irrelevant details and information that the receiver already has. Too much irrelevant information can cloud the main points of a message or cause the receiver to tune out.

A final question you should consider is what are the receiver's preferences in terms of how you deliver your message. For example, does this person generally respond best to information that's presented verbally, in writing, or visually?

Similarly, what communication medium would best suit the receiver? While some people prefer face-to-face conversations, others favor e-mail, the telephone, or other media. A receiver's preference should also affect your strategies for developing your message content.

For example, someone like a manager may want to see how your message fits into the bigger picture. Someone else who needs help in solving a problem is likely to appreciate a narrower focus.

Strategically, you should also consider the receiver's preference when it comes to how you frame your message. One person may respond best to information presented in story or anecdote form. Another could take in information best when you speak to his emotions. A third person might absorb information best in the form of facts and figures.

Once you know enough about the intended receiver, you can tailor your message so it has the maximum impact.

**Question**

You want to ask one of your busiest clients for feedback regarding your company's performance. Before sending your message, you analyze the receiver.

Match the questions to the information they can draw out. Each answer may match with more than one question.

**Options:**

A. Which presentation style makes the most effective impact on the receiver?

B. What information does the receiver have?

C. What information does the receiver require?

D. What are the receiver's interests?

**Targets:**

1. The reader responds best to predesigned formats, such as surveys

2. The receiver has liaised with you throughout the year, and has access to all the information about projects that you've done for his company this year

3. The receiver is a middle manager at his company

**Answer:**

If you know which presentation style makes the biggest impact on the receiver, you can choose a style that will be most effective in drawing out his feedback.

If the receiver has a history of working with you, he will have a good knowledge level and can respond constructively to your request. If the receiver does not have this history, or cannot access the information, you will need to provide the missing information in your request.

If you know the receiver's level, you can tailor the message so that you can ask about his own areas of interest.

# PLANNING THE CONTEXT

**Planning the context**

To communicate effectively, you need to match the communication medium and context to your target receiver. Sometimes your choice of media may be dictated by workplace conventions. In other cases, the two main factors to consider are the importance of the message and the receiver. The importance of a message will help determine factors such as the required impact of the message, the most appropriate presentation style, the need for interactivity, and the importance of information retention.

**Required impact**

Most often, you should communicate important messages via personal, high-impact media – such as phone calls or face-to-face conversations. For less important messages, you can use lower-impact media, such as e-mail, fax, or a letter.

**Presentation style**

You should present formal messages through equally formal media, such as letters or meetings in person. For an important message that must be visually engaging, a visual presentation may be the most appropriate. You can use e-mail, telephone, text messages, and other more casual media for informal communications that don't require high-quality presentation.

**Interactivity**

If your message requires instant feedback or ongoing dialog, you should use highly interactive media, such as face-to-face conversation, the telephone, or instant messaging. For messages that are more one-sided, you can use letters, posters, and other one-way communications media.

**Information retention**

If it's very important for the receiver to retain your message, you should consider using multiple types of media. This can help reinforce your message.

For example, you could communicate your message over the phone, and then send an e-mail that reinforces your message with both text and graphics.

As well as considering the nature and importance of your message, you should use your analysis of the receiver to determine which communication medium or combination of media will be most effective.

For example, if you need to convey a concept to a graphic designer, the best medium to use might be a sample picture or a rough sketch of an image you want this person to design. For someone who typically responds best to information in text form, like a writer, you could use an e-mail or letter.

Sometimes the importance of a message and the characteristics of the receiver make it logical to use two different types of media to convey your message. For example, you've been asked to train a new employee in your department. One essential medium of instruction is hands-on training, where you sit with the new employee and explain the different aspects of the work.

However, you notice that the new employee also likes to learn on his own. To cater for this preference, you can give him training documents that he can read through himself. This enables him to take in the material more comprehensively than he would with just hands-on training.

When it comes to communication planning, many variables will be beyond your control. For example, perhaps you can't determine which medium the receiver would prefer. And, if the receiver is not paying attention to you, you can't force the person to concentrate. However, there are many contextual variables that you can plan, prior to communicating. The most important of these are setting and timing.

**Setting**

Setting refers to the physical environment in which you communicate the message. As much as possible, you should choose a place that is appropriate for the situation. For example, if you need to ask your manager for more information on a financial report, don't ask when you're out of the office, at the company's end of year function. Instead, ask when you're back in the office and your manager has the information at hand.

**Timing**

Timing refers to when you communicate the message. You should try to communicate at a time that is most conducive to positive results. For example, if you need a colleague to help you with a difficult task the following

Monday afternoon, don't tell her about it late on Friday afternoon, when she's packing up to go home. You should wait until Monday morning, when she's more alert and focused on work.

### Case Study: Question 1 of 2
### Scenario

For your convenience, the case study is repeated with each question.

You're a sales manager at a marketing company. You're trying to secure a project to promote a major sporting event, which begins in six months' time. The project is critical to your company, so you want to make your best effort to convince the client – who is located in your city – to choose your company over other promoters.

Plan the best way to communicate your sales pitch by answering the questions in the given order.

### Question

Which medium is best for the situation?

### Options:

1. A telephone call
2. A formal in-person presentation
3. An e-mailed proposal
4. A DVD that combines a written report with full color graphics and animation

### Answer:

Option 1: This is an incorrect option. A phone call could certainly add a personal touch to your sales pitch, but it is not the most effective medium to present your case. A phone call would not give you an opportunity to visually impress the client.

Option 2: This is the correct option. A formal presentation gives you the opportunity to communicate

## Interpersonal Communication

your sales pitch in a high-impact format. It's also a more personal approach, because it enables you to discuss matters in person with the client.

Option 3: This option is incorrect. An e-mailed proposal would give you the opportunity to put your case across in words and visuals, however, it is too impersonal a medium for the importance of this message.

Option 4: This option is incorrect. Even a fancy presentation with animation in DVD format is not as good as a face-to-face interaction in this type of situation. You need a medium that allows two-way interaction and feedback from the receiver.

### Case Study: Question 2 of 2

Which plan of action outlines the best setting and timing for the communication?

**Options:**

1. Schedule a meeting at the client's offices for the following week
2. Schedule a meeting at your offices one month before the sporting event
3. Schedule a lunchtime meeting at a fancy restaurant for the following day

**Answer:**

Option 1: This is the correct option. Presenting your case at the client's offices makes things comfortable and convenient for the client, while also giving you the opportunity to meet potential stakeholders. Setting the meeting for the following week gives you enough time to prepare a presentation and gives you time to carry out the promotional work, should you secure the project.

Option 2: This option is incorrect. Although your offices are a suitable venue for the presentation, holding the meeting one month before the event is far too late, because promotion work needs to begin at least three months before the event.

Option 3: This is an incorrect option. A restaurant is too informal and noisy a setting to present your case. Additionally, the meeting time is too soon because, as a courtesy, you should not ask the client to meet on such short notice.

# SECTION 3 - DELIVERING YOUR MESSAGE AND GETTING FEEDBACK

**SECTION 3 - Delivering Your Message and Getting Feedback**

To plan and deliver a message effectively, you need to ensure that the message is concise and logical, structured using an appropriate strategy, and targeted based on your analysis of the receiver. You should then deliver it at a time and in a setting you've identified as the most appropriate.

You conclude the communication process by getting feedback to verify that the receiver has understood your message. To do this, you first observe the receiver's initial responses. To probe deeper, ask the receiver questions about the message. Finally, if necessary, ask the receiver to summarize your message.

# PLANNING AND DELIVERING A MESSAGE

**Planning and delivering a message**

It's important to set up your communication by first analyzing your receiver, and then planning the context of your message. However, even with this foundation, your communication is likely to fail if you don't plan your message carefully and then deliver it in an effective manner. As a starting point, when targeting your message, it's important to avoid being too wordy or vague. A message must be clear, concise, and logical to be effective. Wherever possible, the message should get right to the point.

As well as ensuring your message is clear and well-structured, you need to target it based on your analysis of the receiver. In other words, your message should reflect the receiver's responsibilities and interests, knowledge level, and preferences. Your message won't be effective if it's not relevant to the receiver, or you pitch it at a level that is too high or too low.

**Question**

## Interpersonal Communication

A new employee, who is a technical novice, is having trouble with job-specific software. He has requested assistance from the company's computer technician. To learn more about the case before visiting the employee, the technician writes the employee an e-mail.

Which message is appropriate for the receiver?

**Options:**

1. This has happened before. What DLLs are missing? What does the installation log say? Get me the information by 3:00 p.m. today. I don't work on these issues without the background information.

2. Scott has had the same problem before. Ask him to help you get a list of the missing dynamic link library (DLL) files, as well as the program's installation log. It shouldn't take more than five minutes.

3. We've had this kind of trouble before. Please send me a list of the missing DLLs, as well as the installation log.

**Answer:**

Appropriate messages show sensitivity or acknowledgement of the receiver's interests and knowledge level.

Option 1: This option is incorrect. Through using terms the receiver may not understand, this message is pitched beyond the receiver's knowledge level. The message also ignores the receiver's interests, because it focuses on the sender's preferences, and makes a demand that the receiver would be unable to fulfil.

Option 2: This is the correct option. With its explanation of terms, this message considers the receiver's lack of knowledge. It also considers the receiver's interests – by explaining how to get the necessary information.

Option 3: This option is incorrect. The receiver likely won't know what the DLLs and installation log are, so this message is pitched higher than the receiver's knowledge level. Also, the receiver cannot easily fulfil the request – so the message ignores the receiver's interests.

Your message should also be shaped using an appropriate strategy so that it's easy for the receiver to follow. Depending on the message content, the situation, and the receiver, you may choose one of four common strategies – moving from what's most to least critical, outlining a problem and then its solution, moving from the big to the small picture, or comparing or contrasting points.

**Most to least critical**

It's useful to order information from most to least important if your message must outline a set of points of differing priorities. In explaining requirements to a job candidate, for example, it makes sense to outline critical requirements in terms of skills and experience first. You may then mention general preferences, or skills that would be useful but aren't strictly required.

**Problem to solution**

If your message addresses specific problems, it's useful to outline each problem and then follow it up with the solution you're proposing. For example, you've patched up several security loopholes in the client's web site. Your message would list each of the security problems, and then explain what you've done to fix them.

**Big to small picture**

It's useful to begin by outlining the big picture, especially if you're addressing a high-level executive or manager. You can then cover the smaller details, explaining how these relate to the bigger picture. For example, you might begin a sales pitch to a corporate manager by outlining an efficiency problem that affects the organization. You could then explain what the product does and how it could improve organizational efficiency.

**Compare or contrast**

Comparing or contrasting situations can strengthen your message by relating what you're suggesting to other situations or events. If you're proposing a project, for example, you might compare it to a similar project that had significant benefits in the past. Or you might contrast it with a project that failed, explaining how your project differs and why it's likely to succeed.

**Question**

Match each strategy for structuring a message to the situation in which its use is most appropriate.

**Options:**

A. Most to least critical

B. Problem to solution

C. Big to small picture

D. Compare or contrast

**Targets:**

1. You need to outline customer requirements to a product development team

2. You want to suggest a strategy for improving poor performance to a team of sales representatives

3. You want to propose a change in a manufacturing process to company executives

4. You want to suggest adopting a new advertising strategy that has worked well for one of your company's competitors

**Answer:**

The most critical to least critical strategy is useful when you need to outline a number of factors, each differing in priority. With the development team, it would be appropriate to outline customers' most important requirements before moving on to those that are less important, or that are simply preferences.

The problem to solution strategy is useful if you need to propose a solution to a specific problem. You might begin by outlining specific problems with a team's performance and then propose a viable solution.

The big to small picture strategy is useful when you're addressing executives, who need to view proposals in terms of their broad effects on an organization. You could describe how the changes to the process will reduce errors or redundancy, and then move on to details about the change you're suggesting.

You can use the compare or contrast strategy to draw similarities between your situation and another situation. You might point out your competitor's success in using a specific advertising strategy when arguing that your company should use a similar approach.

After shaping and targeting your message, you're ready to deliver it to the receiver you've analyzed. You should do this at a time and in a setting you've identified as appropriate.

If you're speaking to the receiver in person or via video link-up, you need to pay particular attention to your presentation. Make good eye contact and speak clearly, at a volume and tempo that's easily understood. Also ensure that your body language is appropriate – sit or stand upright and don't slouch, for example.

# GETTING FEEDBACK

**Getting feedback**

The last stage in the communication process is verifying that the receiver has understood your message. You do this by getting feedback from the receiver. Getting appropriate feedback can involve up to three steps. First pay attention to the receiver's initial responses. Then, if necessary, ask follow-up questions. Finally, you can ask the receiver to provide a summary of your message for you to confirm.

**1. Check initial feedback**

Sometimes you can obtain all the feedback you need from your receiver's initial verbal responses and body language. These may confirm that your message has been fully understood.

**2. Ask questions**

If the receiver has not given much feedback during your message delivery, check the receiver's understanding by asking questions related to the message.

**3. Ask for summary**

If, after step 2, you're still not sure that the receiver fully understands your message, ask the receiver to summarize your message. This will show whether the message has been correctly understood.

Adam is a newly appointed online journalist. His team leader, Wendy, is explaining the process for posting news stories. Follow along as Wendy gets feedback from Adam.

**1. Responses:** During the training session, Adam is slumped in his chair. He periodically responds by nodding his head or saying "OK."

*Adam is bored.*

**2. Questions:** To check Adam's understanding of the web site approval process, Wendy asks him whether he's clear on how stories are approved. Adam responds with "Yes...I think so."

*Adam is uncertain.*

**3. Summary:** Wendy's not certain that Adam has been paying attention to the final piece of training. She asks him to repeat the steps of the web site approval process. Adam stumbles over his response, failing to repeat the steps accurately.

*Adam is not confident.*

In this case, Wendy followed three steps to get feedback from Adam. His final response told her that he had not absorbed the message. So Wendy knows that she needs to communicate it again, this time making sure that Adam is paying attention.

**Question**

You've just relayed some important instructions to Tim, a senior team member. His body language indicates that he didn't fully comprehend the message. You then ask

## Interpersonal Communication

Tim a question, but you're still not certain that he has understood the message completely.

What should you do next?

**Options:**

1. Ask Tim more questions to probe his understanding

2. Observe Tim's body language to see if he appears to have understood the message

3. Ask Tim to summarize your message in his own words

**Answer**

Option 1: This option is incorrect. If Tim's answers don't convince you that he fully understands your message, asking more questions will probably result in the same, unsure responses.

Option 2: This is an incorrect option. Tim's body language is an early indicator of his understanding of the message. But if you're still not sure that Tim fully understands your message at this stage, you should ask him to summarize your message.

Option 3: This is the correct option. If you're still not sure that Tim understands the message after asking questions to check his understanding, you should ask him to summarize your message.

# CHAPTER 3 - LISTENING ESSENTIALS

**CHAPTER 3 - Listening Essentials**
SECTION 1 - The Value and Challenge of Effective Listening
SECTION 2 - Techniques for Active Listening
SECTION 3 - The Role of Feedback in Active Listening

# SECTION 1 - THE VALUE AND CHALLENGE OF EFFECTIVE LISTENING

**SECTION 1 - The Value and Challenge of Effective Listening**

The ability to listen well is a valuable skill that can help you achieve your business and communication goals, prevent mistakes and the need to redo work, improve relationships and morale in the workplace, and facilitate problem solving.

Being aware of the barriers to effective listening can help you overcome them. These barriers include distractions in your work environment, your emotional reactions, your ulterior motives, the speed gap that exists between speaking and thinking, and assumptions you form about what a speaker is trying to say.

# BENEFITS OF EFFECTIVE LISTENING

**Benefits of effective listening**

Jennifer, who runs a catering company, was asked to create a wedding cake. She didn't listen properly to the client though, because she was expecting an important call and kept checking her cell phone. It's now the day of the wedding and the team has created a beautiful white cake. When the client arrives, it turns out that she had ordered a pink cake to fit in with the theme of the wedding. The client is furious and refuses to pay.

Jennifer didn't only fail to listen – she missed an opportunity to develop her image as a top-quality wedding caterer. She may also have damaged her reputation as a good manager. Her team may second guess her next set of instructions, creating friction and compromising the quality of the team's work. A cycle or culture of poor listening can develop into a spiral of more mistakes and misunderstandings. Jennifer must therefore ensure that this was the first and last time that she – or anyone at her company – failed to listen to a client or colleague.

Listening effectively to your colleagues and clients is beneficial in a number of ways. It helps you achieve your business and communication goals. It prevents mistakes that make it necessary to redo work, and it facilitates problem solving. It can also improve your relationships with clients and coworkers, resulting in improved morale and productivity.

**Achieve business and communication goals**

People who listen well are more likely to work well with others and to succeed in their objectives. This is because understanding others and getting to the heart of issues is often necessary before you can move forward with solutions. Listening well helps ensure you're able to secure consensus on issues that affect everyone.

Similarly, you need to understand a client's problem before you can provide a solution. Listening effectively can help to win customers by demonstrating that you care about their needs, and satisfied clients build your company's reputation. When you listen effectively, you portray a positive personal image that impresses customers, superiors, and employees alike – potentially leading to promotions and perks for you.

**Prevent mistakes and rework**

Most mistakes and misunderstandings are due to poor listening, and are avoidable. Listening to what's expected of you translates to better quality work, with fewer false starts. By listening effectively, you save time and money by preventing mistakes in the first place.

**Facilitate problem solving**

Listening effectively helps to facilitate problem solving in the workplace. When someone feels they've been listened to and understood, they'll generally be more willing to cooperate, share information, and voice their opinions or worries in the future. And when you know all the facts, it's easier to find solutions.

**Improve relationships and morale**

Listening well to your clients and your team members helps develop strong professional relationships. When you listen to the ideas and opinions of others, you show that you value what they have to say. This makes others feel more fulfilled and motivated, and improves levels of trust, respect, and cooperation. It can also improve the quality of work done and lead to lower turnover rates.

When they think about improving their communication skills, most people pay far too little attention to their ability to listen. But listening well is one of the most powerful ways to succeed in the workplace. As with any skill, it can require some practice – but the rewards are worth it.

**Question**

What are the benefits of effective listening?

**Options:**

1. Helps to reduce turnover in the workplace
2. Helps you get your points across to employees
3. Helps to build your personal success at work
4. Helps to prevent false starts
5. Reduces the time wasted when other people talk about themselves
6. Enables you to find effective solutions to problems

**Answer:**

Option 1: This is a correct option. Listening to employees helps to make them feel valued and improves morale. This means employees are happier in their work and less likely to leave.

Option 2: This is an incorrect option. Effective listening is about letting other people speak and making sure that you fully understand what they're saying, rather than about getting your points across.

Option 3: This is a correct option. Good listeners are often well liked and successful because they take the time to pay attention to those around them. Also, they're more likely to meet business goals while avoiding mistakes.

Option 4: This is a correct option. By listening carefully to what's expected of you, you're less likely to make mistakes that would otherwise result in rework.

Option 5: This is an incorrect option. Effective listening helps build relationships based on trust and respect. It also helps foster an environment in which people feel safe expressing themselves.

Option 6: This is a correct option. By listening closely to the concerns of all involved, you'll uncover information which might have remained hidden. And solutions will become more apparent.

# OVERCOMING LISTENING BARRIERS

**Overcoming listening barriers**

You've probably experienced the frustration of trying to talk to someone who wasn't listening properly. Poor listeners often tune out or get distracted by their surroundings. They also often interrupt before letting you finish. Poor listeners may jump in with emotional reactions or their own unrelated concerns before hearing you out.

They might not listen properly because they're too focused on mentally preparing their own responses to what you've said so far. Or they may interrupt because they assume they already know what you're going to say, and finish your sentences for you. Besides being annoying, their assumptions aren't always right.

They tune out when listening to a poor speaker or if the subject is boring to them. They may also pay attention only to superficial facts, rather than to the real meaning or intent of a message. It can be difficult to listen properly to someone else. Some of the reasons we struggle to listen properly to other people are distractions, emotions, ulterior motives, the speed gap, and our own assumptions.

The modern work environment is full of distractions. Daily demands sometimes make it hard to slow down enough to focus on a conversation. It's especially difficult to pay attention when you use technologies like the phone or videoconferencing. These don't provide the visual cues of face-to-face conversation, which would normally hold your attention and stop you from trying to multitask.

Your emotional reaction to certain people or information can be a listening barrier. You may react too quickly or strongly when someone has an opinion that you disagree with, or tells you something that makes you anxious. This can lead to poor listening, and even to arguments.

Sometimes red flag words can momentarily distract you so you're unable to pay attention to what a speaker is saying.

**Question**

What do you think the term "red flag word" refers to?

**Options:**

1. A word that evokes a strong emotional reaction
2. A rude or inappropriate word
3. A word intended to provoke the listener

**Answer**

Option 1: This is the correct option. Red flag words are those that provoke a strong emotional reaction in the listener, whether or not the speaker intended this.

Option 2: This option is incorrect. Red flag words aren't necessarily rude or inappropriate – they're simply words that provoke an emotional reaction in you. For example, they may do this because of associations you've developed through your own experiences.

Option 3: This option is incorrect. Red flag words might seem inappropriate to you, but they aren't necessarily meant to provoke or upset you. Often they evoke a strong emotional reaction the speaker didn't intend.

Everyone has different experiences, beliefs, and personalities. So some words or topics might evoke an emotional reaction in you that the speaker didn't intend. These red flags can often lead to misunderstandings.

It's also difficult to be patient and to listen properly to what someone is saying if you don't have complete respect for them. Your body language may give the impression that you don't care about what the speaker is saying or that you've already made some judgement about what they are going to say.

Your ulterior motives can prevent you from giving a speaker your full attention. For example, if you're trying to impress the speaker or influence this person in some way, you'll be too absorbed in planning what you'll say next to really listen. People are often unaware of these underlying desires, which can make it difficult to overcome them.

For example, even trying to be helpful can be a barrier to effective listening, especially if it causes you to interrupt to give advice or finish speakers' sentences for them. Another example of an ulterior motive is trying to compete with the speaker. If a listener feels compelled to challenge every point the speaker makes, the focus on really listening will be lost – and a conversation can easily snowball into an argument.

## Interpersonal Communication

People are capable of processing information three or four times faster than they can talk. During this time delay – or speed gap – it's easy for listeners to get distracted or let their minds wander. Rather than using this time to understand what a speaker is saying, they jump to conclusions and prepare their responses – before the speaker has finished.

Another barrier to effective listening is making assumptions about what the speaker is going to say. A common result of the speed gap is that you feel you know what is coming next in a conversation. You might get impatient and interrupt, try to finish the speaker's sentence, or even disagree before the speaker has finished.

Interrupting like this gives the impression that you don't value what the speaker is saying. When this happens, it's likely to frustrate, confuse, or upset the speaker.

**Question**

Match each of the examples to the types of listening barriers they represent.

**Options:**

A. Amy thinks faster than Jeremy speaks, so she plans her lunch while he's still speaking

B. While on the phone with her boss, Molly reads an e-mail

C. Richard just lost his uncle to cancer and gets angry when Kelly talks about smoking

D. Terry is hoping to be promoted and nods approvingly at everything his boss says

E. Joanne shows how smart she thinks she is by completing other people's sentences

**Targets:**

1. Speed gap

2. Distraction
3. Emotion
4. Ulterior motives
5. Assumptions

**Answer**

The speed gap refers to the fact that you can think faster than a speaker can talk. In that gap, it can be tempting to think ahead rather than focusing on what the speaker is still saying.

Multitasking distracts your attention from a conversation and can cause you to miss important information. Distractions are a common barrier to effective listening.

Some words or topics can evoke an emotional reaction that's not intended by the speaker. These red flags can momentarily prevent the listener from paying full attention to what the speaker is saying.

Ulterior motives, such as your own desires to impress or influence others, can distract you from the goal of simply listening to everything a speaker is trying to say.

When you assume you know what someone is trying to say and you interrupt, the speaker may feel frustrated or undervalued. You may also find that your assumptions are incorrect.

Knowing the types of barriers that exist is a significant step in becoming an effective listener. You need to make a conscious effort to be aware of the distractions in your environment, of your emotions and what triggers them, and of any underlying or ulterior motives you may have. You should also make an effort to control the mental processing you do during the speed gap, and your assumptions about what people are trying to say.

### Distractions in the environment

You should be aware of pressures and distractions in your work environment. This can help you make a conscious effort to tune them out and focus on what a speaker is saying. If possible, move your conversation to an environment with fewer distractions. If you spend a lot of time on the phone, try not to multitask at the same time. Instead focus on what the speaker is saying and show that you're paying attention.

### Emotions and triggers

Try to be aware that some words or topics may have emotional importance for you that they don't for other people. When you feel yourself reacting to something someone has said, ask yourself whether it is a red flag word, and whether the speaker really meant to upset you. Even if you feel you lack respect for the speaker, focus on the overall message and give this person the benefit of the doubt.

### Ulterior motives

It can be difficult to overcome your motives and desires to impress, influence, or help other people. Rather than denying these motives– which can simply drive them beneath the surface – take note of them and ensure that they don't compromise your ability to listen well to others.

### Speed gap

The speed gap can make it difficult to concentrate on what someone is saying. Take note when you find your mind wandering – try to focus on what the person is saying by going over what they've said, or by paying attention to their body language and tone of voice for more information.

### Assumptions

Be aware that you may be making assumptions about things the speaker has not even said. Make sure you let others finish everything they want to say before you respond to their messages.

**Question**

Gloria gets irritable with colleagues who speak slowly and often interrupts them mid-sentence. She also gets annoyed whenever her colleagues mention their personal lives, which she finds tedious. Her job involves a lot of teamwork, but people have started avoiding her – which means her projects are often flawed or late. She realizes that her poor listening skills are starting to interfere with her performance.

What are some of the things Gloria could do to overcome the specific barriers she struggles with?

**Options:**

1. Make a mental note of the topics or words that irritate her

2. Politely ask her colleagues to avoid certain topics when they're around her

3. Allow any speaker to finish before formulating her response

4. Focus on the message rather than on how she feels about the speaker

5. Think carefully about what she wants to say before she interrupts

**Answer:**

Option 1: This is a correct option. Gloria seems to have some red flags that evoke strong emotional reactions. When people talk about their personal lives, Gloria should make a special effort not to get annoyed or angry.

Option 2: This is an incorrect option. Gloria should respect that other people have different cares and worries than she does and allow them to express themselves. She should make note of the topics that irritate her and try not to lash out.

Option 3: This is a correct option. Gloria should resist the urge to interrupt and wait for people to finish before responding to ensure she understands their meaning.

Option 4: This is a correct option. Gloria should focus on what others say rather than giving in to irritability, which will compromise her ability to listen effectively.

Option 5: This is an incorrect option. Gloria should avoid interrupting – and she should let another person finish speaking before she formulates a response. This will ensure she doesn't miss important information or cause offense.

# SECTION 2 - TECHNIQUES FOR ACTIVE LISTENING

**SECTION 2 - Techniques for Active Listening**

There are four levels of listening: non-listening, passive listening, evaluative listening, and active listening. Active listening is the only level at which truly effective communication can occur.

Techniques you can use to listen actively include giving the speaker your full attention, demonstrating your attention to and reception of the message, using the speed gap constructively, and providing the speaker with appropriate feedback.

# FOUR LEVELS OF LISTENING

**Four levels of listening**

You may spend much of your time talking with others, but how much do you actually spend on listening? It's important to remember that hearing and listening are not the same thing.

**Hearing**

Hearing is the passive process of registering sound, without necessarily interpreting or reacting to the information.

**Listening**

Listening is the active process of receiving and interpreting information that's sent to you.

There are four levels of listening, each with different characteristics. They are non-listening, passive listening, evaluative listening, and active listening. Non-listening is the lowest listening level. Non-listeners aren't paying attention at all – they may not even be hearing the words you say.

Someone who daydreams during a meeting is a classic example of a non-listener. This person can't be listening because their attention is entirely on something other than the person speaking. Passive listening is close to non-listening, but the listener is paying slight attention. Passive listeners register words, but not intent or meaning. They are easily distracted and focus on deriving only the bottom line from a message.

Passive listeners appear to pay attention but don't. This can cause misunderstandings and conflict, especially because you may think passive listeners have understood what you've said when in fact they haven't.

The third level of listening is evaluative listening. Evaluative listeners pay attention to your words, but miss subtle cues such as tone and body language. They may be able to repeat your basic message back to you, but miss the difference between what you say and what you mean.

The fourth level of listening is active listening. When you listen actively, you focus on understanding the total message – not just the words that are spoken. Active listening is the only level that can lead to full understanding and effective communication. It requires effort and concentration, but its benefits can include better communication, higher morale, and improved productivity.

**Question**

In a meeting, Rosa discusses a possible move to new premises with her team. She outlines the reasons why a move has been suggested but indicates her reservations about the idea through her facial expression and tone of voice.

Match each level of listening to the scenario in which it's occurring.

**Options:**

A. Non-listening
B. Passive listening
C. Evaluative listening
D. Active listening

**Targets:**

1. Dean is daydreaming. He's paying no attention to the speaker.

2. Terence fades in and out of the conversation during the meeting. He pays closest attention when a decision is reached.

3. Pam pays attention to what Rosa says but doesn't realize Rosa is hesitant about the move.

4. Carmen pays attention to Rosa's message and body language. She shows she's attentive and asks Rosa why she's hesitant about the move.

**Answer:**

Dean is focused on himself. He isn't listening at all, so he has no idea what Rosa is saying. This is an example of non-listening.

Terence is barely paying attention and is focused only on deriving the bottom line of Rosa's message. This is an example of passive listening.

Pam listened to what Rosa said, but not to how she said it. She failed to understand Rosa's hesitation about the move because she didn't read subtle cues in her body language and tone of voice. This is an example of evaluative listening.

Carmen paid full attention to both the verbal and nonverbal content of Rosa's message, with the result that she understood it fully and was able to respond appropriately. This is an example of active listening.

# ACTIVE LISTENING TECHNIQUES

**Active listening techniques**

There are four key techniques you must master to be an active listener. You need to give 100% of your attention to the speaker, demonstrate your attention to and reception of the message, use the speed gap constructively, and provide the speaker with appropriate feedback.

Giving 100% of your attention is difficult because often you're surrounded by distractions. These can take the form of internal factors like feeling hot or being hungry. Or they can be external factors like a noisy environment or a speaker with an accent that's hard to understand. It's vital you learn to block out all distractions to prevent misunderstandings from occurring.

As an active listener, your goal should be to understand and connect with people. This means paying attention to the words used, and to how they are spoken.

Three techniques can help ensure you don't become distracted when listening:
- make a conscious decision to listen actively so that you fully understand what the speaker is saying,

- stop what you're doing and focus completely on the speaker, and
- pay full attention to the words, tone, and body language of the speaker.

**Make a conscious decision to listen**

The first step in listening actively is recognizing that what others have to say is as important as what you say to them, and making a conscious decision to listen. Once you have fully understood what someone else has said, you can reply with your ideas.

**Stop what you're doing**

It's very difficult to speak properly to someone who appears to be only half listening and who, for example, continues typing or looking in another direction as you talk. When someone begins speaking, you should stop what you are doing so that you can focus completely on this person. This shows that you value the person's contribution and are prepared to hear them out. In turn, this builds trust and rapport, and will encourage the speaker to communicate more clearly and fully.

**Pay attention**

Willing yourself to concentrate on the speaker helps you maintain focus and stops you from becoming distracted. You should pay close attention to both the words and body language of a speaker. Cues like posture, tone, and facial expression can give you important information that a person's words alone don't convey.

Communication is a two-way process. When you listen, it's important to give responses demonstrating that you're really paying attention to and receiving the information presented. This prevents misunderstandings from occurring and builds rapport. It also keeps you open to new information – if you behave attentively, you'll absorb and retain new information better.

You can show your involvement in a conversation in two ways:
- by using verbal responses, and
- by using nonverbal responses.

**Verbal responses**

Verbal responses are things you say. They can be as simple as "Uh huh" or "Tell me more," or they can indicate a reaction to the message, such as "Wow!" or "Interesting." Providing verbal responses demonstrates that you are listening, and encourages the speaker to continue expressing their points.

**Nonverbal responses**

Nonverbal responses are things you do. For example, nodding and showing appropriate emotion in your face can reassure a speaker that you're listening. One important guideline is to face a speaker when you listen. This makes it easy for you to pick up on the speaker's body language, as well as enabling you to show interest and engagement – for example, by leaning slightly forward and making eye contact. Your facial reactions should match the emotional content of the speaker's message, to show that you're detecting how the speaker feels.

It's important be aware of your body language and to keep your verbal and nonverbal responses in sync.

For example, if you frown and cross your arms while saying that you agree with someone, you'll be sending a mixed message that's likely to lead to tension or distrust. This is because your words and body are sending conflicting signals.

Interpersonal Communication

The term "speed gap" refers to the fact that people think faster than they speak. As a listener, your thoughts can easily run ahead of a speaker's words. This is part of what makes it easy to become distracted while listening. However, this gap can also give you the opportunity to analyze a speaker's full message and its meaning. Learning to make good use of the speed gap is a vital part of active listening.

You can use the speed gap to do three constructive things when listening:
- exercise emotional control – identify and restrain your own emotions,
- pay attention to the speaker's body language so that you pick up the nonverbal component of this person's message, and
- structure the speaker's message by taking mental notes, or even written notes when appropriate.

Exercising emotional control is vital to active listening, but it's hard to master. We all have beliefs and values that are important to us. If a speaker says something that conflicts with our views, it can arouse our emotions and cause us to lose focus.

To remain in control of your emotions when a speaker says something that you disagree with or find upsetting, you should take four steps:
- recognize your reaction and what has triggered it
- delay your response so you have time to consider it carefully
- practice empathy by focusing on what you have in common instead of on what divides you from the speaker, and

- evaluate ideas rationally and focus on what's expressed, rather than on who expressed it or how they did so.

**Recognize your reaction**

Signals that you're upset include flushing, breathing faster, and a strong desire to interrupt. It's important to recognize when this is happening so that you can refrain from responding in anger.

**Delay your response**

Take a deep breath and count to ten. This gives you time to think and to calm down if you're upset.

**Practice empathy**

Showing empathy involves demonstrating that you're aware of the speaker's feelings and experiences. You're empathetic when instead of focusing on your own feelings, you put yourself in the speaker's position. Understanding the other person's point of view helps you stay calm and keeps you from judging that person's ideas prematurely.

**Evaluate ideas rationally**

Before you evaluate an idea, you must first understand it – or you risk missing the point and reacting inappropriately. This is vital when you are upset because emotions can cloud your judgment unless you control them carefully.

As well as giving you time to control your emotional reactions, the speed gap is useful because it gives you enough time to pick up the nonverbal cues speakers send out. Body language affects the meaning of the words we say. Posture, tone, facial expression – these can all add to or even alter the meaning of a spoken message.

For example, a manager may have to deliver an unpleasant message to an employee about potential layoffs. The employee should scrutinize the manager's behavior. Is she smiling? Does she look concerned? These clues affect the employee's interpretation of the message.

A third constructive way to use the speed gap is to structure the information you receive. There are three techniques you can use to help do this:
- indexing and noting points,
- sequencing list items or steps in a procedure, and
- comparing what the speaker is saying to what this person has already said.

**Indexing**

When you practice indexing, you outline a speaker's ideas by noting main points and subpoints. This is excellent for improving your retention of the information that's delivered. For example, taking notes during a meeting with a colleague will ensure that you remember the fundamental points made, as well as making it more likely you'll be able to recall the details associated with each of these points.

**Sequencing**

Sequencing involves structuring information chronologically or in order of action.

**Comparing**

Comparing prevents misunderstandings by enabling you to determine whether the speaker is being consistent and making sense. If something does not add up, you can then seek further clarification.

**Question**

Kim is explaining her company's new pricing policy to Philip.

Which actions indicate that Philip is making good use of the speed gap?

**Options:**
1. Philip watches Kim move, noting changes in her posture and expression
2. Philip halts Kim's presentation to ask about the reasons for the price change
3. Philip becomes upset at the price increase and assumes an angry facial expression
4. Philip mentally matches what Kim is saying to what she said earlier
5. Philip realizes he's annoyed at hearing about the price increase so he takes a deep breath and considers the information that's been presented

**Answer:**
Option 1: This option is correct. Philip is using the time he has because of the speed gap to pick up on the nonverbal component of Kim's message. This will ensure he doesn't miss any information transmitted through Kim's body language or tone.

Option 2: This option is incorrect. Instead of interrupting, Philip should wait until Kim has finished speaking before he requests more information.

Option 3: This is an incorrect option. Philip should use the speed gap to recognize that he's reacting emotionally and to calm himself before responding.

Option 4: This option is correct. Philip is comparing elements of Kim's message to determine whether she's being consistent. This is a good way to use the time provided by the speed gap.

Option 5: This is a correct option. Philip is using the speed gap well to control his emotions and objectively evaluate the ideas that Kim is presenting.

**Question**

## Interpersonal Communication

Gail and Zack are discussing their upcoming performance reviews. Which scenarios illustrate that they pay attention and make constructive use of the speed gap?

**Options:**

1. Zack remains at his desk while Gail speaks, catching up on his e-mails while he listens. When he gets annoyed with something she says, he recognizes his emotion and tells her how irritated he is.

2. Gail stops typing a report and turns to face Zack as he speaks. She meets his gaze and smiles to encourage him to continue speaking.

3. Zack can't understand why Gail shows so much anxiety about the performance review, but he nods and smiles at everything she says anyway.

4. Zack has to leave the office early and asks Gail to send several memos to reviewers by the end of the day. Gail writes down the key points as Zack speaks and makes eye contact with him when she's not writing.

**Answer**

Option 1: This is an incorrect option. Zack isn't paying attention to what Gail is saying, instead allowing himself to be distracted by e-mail messages. He also didn't use the speed gap to give himself time to control his emotions, delay his response, and calm down.

Option 2: This option is correct. Gail has made a conscious decision to listen actively to Zack. She's focused on their interaction and on providing nonverbal responses to let Zack know that she's taking in what he says.

Option 3: This is an incorrect option. Zack isn't trying to empathize with Gail's situation. He seems to respond to her words, but his permanent smile doesn't appropriately reflect her feeling and won't make her feel understood.

Option 4: This is a correct option. Gail is taking down key information and showing her attention by maintaining eye contact with Zack. This will help ensure that she understands the full message and will be able to remember it later.

The final skill you need as an active listener is that of providing feedback. To do this, you ask clarifying questions, reflect feelings without judgment, and prove your understanding of what has been said.

# SECTION 3 - THE ROLE OF FEEDBACK IN ACTIVE LISTENING

## SECTION 3 - The Role of Feedback in Active Listening

Listening actively involves giving a speaker appropriate feedback, to confirm your understanding of both the factual and emotional content of the speaker's message. Strategies for giving feedback include paraphrasing the speaker's message, and asking closed-ended or open-ended questions.

# TYPES OF FEEDBACK

**Types of feedback**

Have you ever tried explaining something to a person who makes no response at all? It can be very disconcerting. You can't tell whether your message is getting through. This can distract you so much that you even lose track of what you're trying to say. At the very least, when you walk away from the conversation, you won't be confident that the other person has grasped what you said.

Effective listening isn't just about passively absorbing information. It's also about actively engaging with the speaker, by giving this person the right feedback. The speaker needs to know that you're listening and that you either do or don't understand the message. There are two main types of feedback you can give as a listener. You use feedback to demonstrate or clarify your understanding of facts. And you use it to clarify or show that you understand the speaker's feelings – the emotional content of this person's message.

**Question**

Do you think it's always important to provide feedback about both the facts and feelings in a speaker's message?

**Options:**

1. Yes
2. No

**Answer**

The nature and content of a speaker's message will determine the type of feedback that's required. Sometimes it's unnecessary to confirm facts because a message is short, simple, and clear, or its purpose is mostly to convey emotion. And sometimes a speaker's message is neutral, so there's no need to respond to emotion.

You should provide feedback about the factual content of a speaker's message if you haven't fully understood the message, it's ambiguous, or it seems incomplete.

For example, if your manager tells you it's important to finish an assignment quickly, you need to establish what's meant by "quickly." When is the assignment actually due?c You should also provide feedback to confirm your understanding of facts if the speaker's message is complex or it's particularly important that you understand it.

For instance, it's a good idea to confirm you've understood the steps in a new work process that a colleague has just explained to you. Feedback about facts isn't needed for short, simple factual messages like "I'm going to take my lunch break now" – or for purely emotional statements, like "I hate being late for meetings."

When part or all of a message is designed to express emotion, it's important to give feedback about the speaker's feelings. Beyond just showing empathy, you do this to encourage people to express themselves fully. In turn, this encourages the flow of information and allows them to release tensions that might otherwise lead to conflict.

If a colleague says something like "I'm sick of being treated like this," for example, he or she expects a response. You should ask about this person's feelings and what has prompted them. You should also demonstrate empathy. Feedback about feelings is unnecessary if a speaker's message is neutral. If your boss mentions in passing that he sent the e-mail he promised, asking how he feels about it obviously wouldn't be appropriate.

Remember that your body language, facial expression, and tone of voice also provide a speaker with feedback. If you express interest verbally but your body language shows you're bored, the speaker will feel you're being dishonest.

**Question**

Which statements require fact or feeling feedback from a listener?

**Options:**

1. "I can't believe he said that to me."

2. "Wow, the day really flew by! Well, I'm heading home. See you tomorrow."

3. "The latest financial report is available in the Annual Reports folder on the network."

4. "You'll need to assemble a team that's big enough to handle this job."

**Answer:**

Option 1: This is a correct option. This statement is designed to convey emotion. You should encourage the speaker to finish explaining what's on his mind.

Option 2: This is an incorrect option. It's clear the speaker is simply glad to be heading home – you don't need to clarify any facts or prompt the person for more information about her feelings.

Option 3: This is an incorrect option. The factual content of this message is simple and clear and you don't need to ask for clarification. The message also isn't designed to convey emotion, so no specific feeling feedback is required.

Option 4: This is a correct option. In response to this statement, you may need to clarify the facts – what's meant by "big enough" and what skills team members must possess, for instance.

# FEEDBACK STRATEGIES

**Feedback strategies**

There are three main types of feedback strategies, each appropriate for different circumstances. The strategies are paraphrasing what the speaker has said, asking closed-ended questions, and asking open-ended questions. When you understand the message, you paraphrase to reflect it back to the speaker. When in doubt, you ask questions to clarify.

**Paraphrasing**

Paraphrasing what the speaker has said involves repeating the message in your own words. This is useful for confirming your understanding of both the facts and feelings conveyed in the message, when you're confident that you've understood them. So paraphrasing reflects the message back to the speaker and indicates that you discerned the intent behind it.

**Closed-ended question**

A closed-ended question is one that has only a limited set of possible short answers, like "yes" or "no," or "2 o'clock." You can use this type of question to clarify a particular fact when you're not sure you've understood the message.

**Open-ended question**

Open-ended questions require more than a simple, brief response. They encourage the speaker to elaborate. These questions are particularly good for clarifying the speaker's feelings when the emotional content of a message is unclear to you. They allow the speaker to expand on what has been said, or to reflect on their feelings or motives.

To determine which feedback to use, first ask yourself if the speaker has delivered a clear message. If so, paraphrase the key content. If not, ask yourself whether the message is largely factual or largely emotional. If factual, ask a closed-ended question to clarify facts. If emotional, ask an open-ended question to clarify feelings.

When you paraphrase, you should focus on repeating only the gist of what the speaker has said – even if you don't agree with the speaker. Your purpose is to ensure you've understood the message by reflecting it back to the speaker. You should express yourself in a way that invites the speaker to correct you if your paraphrasing is inaccurate, or if you've missed the point.

An example of how you might paraphrase is "So the client must sign off twice, before and after graphic development. Is that right?" Or you might say something like "Can I just check that I've understood? What you're saying is..."

Using a closed-ended question to clarify a message, you might ask something like "When you say 'soon,' do you mean by the end of the day?" This invites a brief, targeted answer, like "yes" or "no." Or you could ask "What exactly do you mean by a 'large' team?"

Using an open-ended question to encourage the speaker, you might say something like "I'm not sure I understand. Why are you so upset?" Or you could say "Can you tell me more about that?" To encourage reflection, you might ask "What do you think would have resolved the conflict?"

**Question**

Match examples of feedback types to appropriate circumstances for using them.

**Options:**

A. "Where will the second meeting be held?"

B. "Because the entire team must be trained before the product is released, we'll have to have training finished before launch. Is this correct?"

C. "How would you describe your reaction to her report?"

D. "So you're saying that you're being held responsible for the actions of your manager."

**Targets:**

1. When you've understood the message

2. When you haven't fully understood the message, and need to clarify the feeling behind it

3. When you haven't fully understood the message, and need to clarify factual details

**Answer:**

When you're confident that you've understood the content of the message, you reflect the basic message back to the speaker as a summary. Your paraphrasing may also invite the speaker to verify that you've summarized correctly.

An open-ended question that encourages the speaker to elaborate is best used when you need more information to understand the feeling behind the message.

A closed-ended question that requires a short clarification from the speaker is appropriate when you haven't fully understood the facts of a message.

Knowing when and how to use each type of feedback will enable you to complete the process of active listening. When you provide appropriate feedback, you show the speaker that you're determined to understand what they are telling you.

**Question**

Noel tells Steven about the overtime he has had to put into his team's project, which has been beset by various mistakes and problems. He gets visibly frustrated and angry when he says "And instead of helping me find a solution, my boss has become my biggest problem!" Finally, he lapses into silence.

Which is the best response for Steven to make?

**Options:**

1. "So you're saying the project is in a mess."

2. "You seem quite upset, Noel. What has been happening with your boss?"

3. "Seems it's up to you to pull the team together. When exactly is your deadline?"

**Answer:**

Option 1: This option is incorrect. Paraphrasing what a speaker has said is a useful way to confirm understanding, especially of factual content. In this case though, Steven should prompt Noel for more information about his boss because this is obviously what's upsetting him.

Option 2: This is the correct option. Steven's open-ended question will encourage Noel to provide more information, or at the least to vent some frustration.

Option 3: This option is incorrect. Steven's paraphrase is premature because Noel hasn't said that he's responsible for pulling the team together. A closed-ended question would be useful for finding out a particular piece of information. But there seems to be more to Noel's experience that he isn't sharing. Encouraging him to go further on the subject would give Steven a more complete picture of the problem he's having with his boss.

# CHAPTER 4 - COMMUNICATING ASSERTIVELY

**CHAPTER 4 - Communicating Assertively**
   SECTION 1 - Recognizing Assertive Behavior and Its Benefits
   SECTION 2 - Requirements for Assertive Communication
   SECTION 3 - Communicating Assertively

# SECTION 1 - RECOGNIZING ASSERTIVE BEHAVIOR AND ITS BENEFITS

## SECTION 1 - Recognizing Assertive Behavior and Its Benefits

You are assertive when you express your opinion confidently and positively, speak directly and honestly, remain respectful while expressing your views, and make yourself heard and understood. Being assertive helps you develop good relationships with your colleagues.

Assertive behavior is a win-win situation. Both parties feel good about the encounter – both know that they're respected and they're not wasting their time. There is mutual understanding and respect. Aggressive behavior is overbearing and intimidating, while passive behavior is indirect and submissive. Both are ineffective and have a negative impact on the communicators and their relationship.

# WHAT IS ASSERTIVE BEHAVIOR?

**What is assertive behavior?**

Imagine you're in a meeting and you really want to make a point, but someone else is speaking. You know it's important to assert yourself to ensure your voice is heard. Does this mean you should interrupt loudly to make your point? Or should you sit quietly and wait for a gap in the conversation?

Often people associate the idea of being assertive with behavior that's aggressive or arrogant. For example, you may think of someone who interrupts you to make a point and speaks loudly as asserting himself and his opinion. However, this is aggressive – rather than assertive – behavior.

Behaving assertively isn't about overriding or offending others. It's about communicating clearly and effectively. Behaving assertively means you make use of four main characteristics when communicating with others:

- expressing yourself confidently and positively,

- speaking directly and honestly, rather than hinting or presuming your real meaning will be inferred,
- demonstrating respect for others while expressing your views, and
- communicating in a way that ensures you'll be heard and understood.

**Express yourself confidently**

To be an assertive communicator, you need to express what you think confidently and positively to others. Doing this makes it far more likely that your message will get through.

**Speak directly and honestly**

Speaking honestly and directly involves saying what you really mean and feel. This will also encourage others to be more open, which can help you to develop good relationships. And people will respect your honesty.

**Demonstrate respect**

Demonstrating respect for others and their perspectives while being assertive involves saying what you think or how you feel without offending anyone. This facilitates mutual respect.

**Be heard and understood**

To be assertive, you need to speak your views distinctly enough so that people will listen to and understand you. When others listen to what you say, they're able to take your views or feelings into account.

An assertive attitude is demonstrated through assertive behavior, which takes several forms. In conversation, it involves keeping an open and relaxed posture; speaking in a pleasant, conversational tone; and making appropriate eye contact. It involves participating in the discussion, rather than withdrawing from or dominating it.

Being assertive requires that you maintain awareness and control over your own emotions so that you can express your opinions and views effectively to other people. For example, if you feel you're being treated unfairly, recognizing your feelings and calmly discussing them with your manager is likely to be much more productive than venting your frustration or anger.

Being assertive enables you to deal with different situations easily and efficiently. When you're assertive, you are able to do the following:

- begin, change, and end a topic of conversation without being rude or overriding others,
- express your opinions and feelings honestly so that others can take these into account,
- ask for the cooperation and help of others without feeling guilty or anxious,
- decline requests politely and confidently if you feel they are too demanding or that you won't be able to meet them,
- question rules and guidelines that you feel are unfair and stand up for your own rights, and
- accept compliments and constructive criticism from others.

**Question**

What are typical characteristics of assertive behavior?

**Options:**

1. Expressing yourself confidently and positively
2. Speaking directly and honestly
3. Demonstrating respect for others at all times
4. Ensuring that you're heard and understood

5. Controlling emotions by communicating only facts
6. Ensuring that others agree with your points

**Answer:**

Option 1: This is a correct option. One aspect of being assertive is expressing your opinions confidently and positively. This helps ensure that others will listen to and understand what you have to say.

Option 2: This option is correct. To be assertive, you need to say what you really mean and feel. This encourages others to reciprocate and helps in building good relationships.

Option 3: This is a correct option. An important aspect of assertive behavior is being respectful of others and not causing offense, which can prevent others from listening to you.

Option 4: This option is correct. Being assertive means you speak so that people listen to you, understand you, and take your opinion into account.

Option 5: This is an incorrect option. To communicate assertively, keeping your emotions in control is vital. However, being direct and honest may involve communicating your feelings, as well as pure facts.

Option 6: This option is incorrect. To be assertive, you should focus on getting your points across clearly and ensuring they're understood. But you can't enforce agreement – others won't necessarily agree with you all the time.

# BENEFITS OF ASSERTIVE BEHAVIOR

**Benefits of assertive behavior**

Assertive behavior has benefits not just for the person who's assertive, but for everyone interacting with the assertive person.

When you're the other party in a conversation with someone assertive, these are some of the benefits that you'll experience:
- you feel good about the encounter because the other person listens to your views and shares her opinions with you honestly,
- you feel respected because the assertive person encourages you to share your views, and listens to and respects them,
- you know the interaction won't have wasted your time because each person's contributions have been considered, leading to an effective outcome,
- you understand what's being said because the assertive speaker makes her points clearly and confidently,

- you have space to make your own decisions because an assertive person won't push you into making a decision or tell you how you should feel, and
- you'll be exposed to an effective communication model that you can learn from.

**Question**

Behaving assertively during an interaction is a "win-win" situation for both parties.

You've just learned how you'll benefit from someone else's assertiveness. Now, how do you think you'll benefit if you're the one who behaves assertively?

**Options:**

1. Others will respect you for speaking assertively
2. Colleagues won't disagree with you
3. You'll develop more open and honest relationships
4. You'll be empowered to deal with stressful work situations
5. You'll be able to avoid having to solve problems
6. You'll feel productive and positive
7. You'll achieve what you want more often

**Answer:**

Option 1: This is a correct option. You gain respect when speaking openly and honestly to your colleagues.

Option 2: This option is incorrect. Assertive behavior doesn't involve preventing your colleagues from disagreeing with you. This is aggressive behavior. When you're assertive, you allow others to disagree with you, but you also find a way to ensure they'll listen to you and respect your opinions.

Option 3: This option is correct. By being frank with your colleagues, you encourage others to behave in a similar way. This develops open and honest relationships in the workplace.

Option 4: This is a correct option. Behaving assertively equips you to respond to and resolve difficult work situations, rather than giving in or failing to play an active role, which can lead to frustration.

Option 5: This option is incorrect. Open communication, which results from being assertive, is often a prerequisite for resolving problems in the workplace, rather than avoiding them.

Option 6: This a correct option. If you're assertive, you're confident in what you do, in how you approach your colleagues, and in your abilities. This makes you a productive employee who has a positive attitude toward work and its challenges.

Option 7: This option is correct. By standing up for what you think or feel, communicating clearly, and respecting others, you make it more likely that your ideas will get a favorable response.

Communicating assertively yourself can have these benefits:

- you get what you want or need more often,
- you gain respect from others, for yourself and your position,
- you feel less powerless and so reduce your stress in workplace situations,
- you solve problems more efficiently,
- you feel more productive and positive, and
- you develop more open, honest relationships.

**Get what you want**

Communicating assertively won't mean you always get what you want or need, but it does make this more likely.

If you don't speak up, others often simply won't know your interests or remember to take them into account. Also, by being direct but respectful of others, you make it more likely that they'll react favorably to your requests or opinions. Being assertive may, for example, enable you to secure the resources you need to complete a project on time. It could also help you secure a deserved promotion or salary increase.

**Gain respect**

You'll gain respect, both personally and for your position at work, if others see you as someone who sticks up for your rights and what you believe in. Earning respect is a two-way process. If you clearly value the opinions of other people, they're likely to reciprocate with greater respect for yours.

**Reduce stress**

You resolve problems better when you're assertive. Because you're better able to cope, you'll feel less stressed, helpless, victimized, or irritated in workplace situations. Also, asserting the way you feel about a stressful situation at work can help resolve it. For example, you may let your manager know that you're worried about meeting a deadline because of work pressure. This could result in your being given the extra resources or time you need.

**Solve problems**

Good communication is often at the heart of effective problem solving. By being assertive, you make your own interests clear while also considering those of others. You also clarify the issues more effectively. These characteristics make it much easier to get to the bottom of problems and to identify long-term solutions.

**Feel more productive**

Communicating assertively can improve your satisfaction at work, making you feel more productive and positive. By expressing yourself clearly, you gain a sense of empowerment. You also increase your ability to solve problems and get things done. At the same time, behaving assertively involves respecting the views of others. Because people around you feel valued, you help create a positive and more productive work environment.

**Develop relationships**

Being assertive involves communicating openly and honestly and demonstrating respect for others. In turn, this encourages coworkers to be honest with you. This builds good relationships based on mutual respect.

So being assertive at work has benefits for both you and your colleagues. It helps you get your own views across and solve problems more effectively. It equips you to deal with stressful situations like confrontation, asking for help, or saying "no." At the same time, it enables you to maintain positive, respectful, and productive relationships.

# CLASSIFYING COMMUNICATION BEHAVIOR

**Classifying communication behavior**

People who don't communicate assertively may instead be aggressive, trying to force their points on others and ignoring their views. Or they may be passive – failing to make their own voices heard or hiding what they feel. Both of these approaches have disadvantages for everyone involved.

People who are directly aggressive in the way they communicate are easy to spot. They may interrupt you often or talk over you. They're likely to come across as rude and inconsiderate and may push other people around. Aggressive behaviors include glaring and staring, crossing arms defiantly, invading others' personal space, and speaking loudly.

A variation, which can be less obvious, is passive-aggressive behavior. This involves reacting to others aggressively but not actually expressing the aggression – at least not verbally. For example, someone may use only facial expressions or sarcasm to demonstrate anger or

## Interpersonal Communication

annoyance. This person avoids open conflict but still gets the point across that she's angry or annoyed.

Passive-aggressive people usually intend to get even with the people they disagree with, but not directly. Instead, they hope those people will suffer some consequence of their actions, figure out on their own what they've done wrong, and "learn their lesson." Sometimes, passive-aggressive people will manipulate circumstances or people to make sure their point gets across. Or they'll talk about the problem with other parties instead of with the person they're in disagreement with. What they won't do is confront the problem directly.

In a sales meeting, each person – Rick, Taku, Margaret, and Tom – demonstrate different types of behavior. Follow along as the members discuss a new idea.

**Tom:** So Rick, I believe you've got a good idea that could help us boost sales.

Rick: I do indeed. It's too bland just to offer customers a discount. Instead, why don't we advertise that if customers choose to invest with us, we'll contribute to their favorite charities.

*Rick seems smug and confident.*

**Tom:** Right, so what will that mean we'd have to...

**Rick:** There isn't really anything to think about. What we were offering before as discounts would make up the contributions.

*Rick uses a bold tone of voice, leaning forward and gesturing emphatically.*

**Margaret:** Hmm. I'm not sure...

**Rick:** Oh, you're never sure, Margaret.

*Rick uses a sarcastic tone.*

**Margaret:** Oh, well then.

*Margaret clears her throat and then speaks quietly, narrowing her eyes and looking angrily at Rick.*

**Tom:** Go ahead Margaret. I also have some reservations, and I'd like to hear your ideas.

*Tom is calm and confident.*

**Margaret:** Never mind. We'll go with Rick's idea. But if it doesn't work out, don't blame me.

*Margaret is annoyed.*

After she has been interrupted, Margaret stays silent. However, she occasionally raises her eyes to the ceiling when Rick is talking. Rick continues talking loudly about his ideas, often interrupting Tom, who maintains a calm tone of voice. Taku looks like he has something to say, but he keeps quiet and doesn't contribute anything.

**Question**

Match two of the four team members to the types of behavior they displayed during the meeting.

Which person was directly aggressive and which person was passive-aggressive?

**Options:**

A. Margaret
B. Rick
C. Tom
D. Taku

**Targets:**

1. Directly aggressive
2. Passive–aggressive

**Answer**

In the meeting, Rick was directly aggressive. He interrupted Tom, overriding him to continue presenting his own ideas. He also cut Margaret off and made a sarcastic remark about her.

Margaret demonstrated passive-aggressive behavior. She made it clear she was annoyed through her facial expression, but she didn't verbalize her reaction or contribute her opinion, except to imply Rick would ultimately be proven wrong.

In the meeting, Rick was aggressive, and Margaret exhibited passive–aggressive behavior. Rick's directly aggressive behavior has several disadvantages:

- he's likely to lose the respect of his colleagues, so his behavior may damage his work relationships,
- his intimidating behavior prevents others from expressing their views, so potentially relevant and important points aren't raised, and
- his behavior makes it unlikely that the meeting will have a productive outcome because it prevents other team members from participating in the decision.

Margaret's passive-aggressive behavior also has disadvantages. Because she didn't express her feelings or opinion, she's likely to leave the meeting feeling frustrated and stressed. She also added to the negative tone of the meeting by showing her annoyance rather than contributing her ideas and respecting those of others.

Behaving passively can be just as problematic as being aggressive. It indicates that you're not confident enough to express your opinions or feelings. Very passive people have trouble keeping eye contact. They hesitate to contribute in group discussions and have trouble sticking up for themselves. They often speak softly, slouch, and appear withdrawn.

So whereas an assertive person sticks up for his rights, a passive person is more likely to keep quiet or even accept being pushed around. Often, passive people are trying to avoid confrontation or embarrassment. They want others to like them, so they treat others' needs and wants as more important than their own. But behaving passively can lead to feelings of frustration and helplessness in the long run.

People may behave passively for different reasons and in different ways. Generally, you can classify this behavior as either indirect behavior or giving-in behavior.

**Indirect behavior**

Indirect behavior is characterized by passive communication that is evasive, uncertain, and indecisive. Someone who is indirect lacks the confidence to state his view or say how he feels. Instead he talks around the issue, using weak and unclear language. Or he keeps quiet and doesn't state his opinions at all, often for fear that he'll be unpopular.

**Giving-in behavior**

Someone who gives in passively does so because she's unwilling to say "no." Even if she isn't comfortable doing what is asked, she does it anyway. A person who displays capitulating passive behavior doesn't have the confidence to stand up for her own rights.

Follow along as the members of the sales team continue their discussion of Rick's marketing idea. Again Taku looks a little frustrated, as if he wants to say something.

**Tom:** This idea may face some resistance on the executive front.

*Tom sounds apprehensive.*

**Margaret:** Taku, do you have any thoughts on this?

*Margaret is curiously.*

**Taku:** Er...well, we might want to think about an alternative, but I'm not sure what the group wants. I guess Rick's idea sounds alright.

*Taku sounds unsure.*

**Rick:** Thanks, Taku. Hey, how about you do us a favor? Could you make a pot of coffee for us?

*Rick is flippant.*

**Taku:** Um, well. OK.

*Taku is hesitant at first, but then he's submissive.*

**Rick:** Cheers buddy. Anyway...Tom, why do you think there will be some resistance?

Taku displayed both types of passive behavior. He didn't speak up until he was asked for his thoughts and then he dodged indirectly around the issue rather than stating a clear opinion. When Rick asked Taku to make coffee, it was clear that Taku was uncomfortable with the request. However, he did it anyway. This is giving in.

**Question**

Simon, Beth, Carl, and Jackie are sitting around a table during a break.

Access the Coffee Break learning aid for details about how they communicate and then match everyone to the type of behavior they display.

**Options:**
A. Beth
B. Simon
C. Carl
D. Jackie

**Targets:**
1. Assertive
2. Passive-aggressive
3. Passive

4. Aggressive

**Answer**

Beth communicates confidently and calmly. She politely asks Jackie not to interrupt, which is an example of behaving assertively.

Unlike Beth, Simon doesn't communicate his irritation to the offender, Jackie. Instead, he expresses it to a third party, Beth. This is an example of passive-aggressive behavior.

Carl wants to speak but isn't assertive enough to share his views. This is an example of passive behavior.

Jackie constantly interrupts and talks over other people in a way that's disrespectful, which is an example of aggressive behavior.

# SECTION 2 - REQUIREMENTS FOR ASSERTIVE COMMUNICATION

## SECTION 2 - Requirements for Assertive Communication

Assertive communication has three key requirements: being honest and straightforward, respecting the needs and feelings of others, and using appropriately assertive body language and tone. Being honest and straightforward entails knowing and communicating your emotions, taking ownership of your opinions using "I" statements, avoiding judgments or exaggerations, and using direct language.

Demonstrating respect for others includes starting with a positive statement, showing respect for other viewpoints, and presenting your opinions in a neutral rather than abrasive way. Examples of assertive body language include an upright but relaxed posture and calm demeanor and gestures. A calm but resonant voice with a neutral pitch is appropriate.

# HOW TO BE ASSERTIVE

**How to be assertive**

You want to ask your boss for a raise, which you feel you deserve. Instead, you murmur about the hours you've been putting in and how well your projects are doing, and only hint that you think a raise is in order. The result? You get a pat on the back, but your boss glosses over your side remark about that raise.

To get any message across clearly, it's vital to be assertive when you communicate. But how do you do this?

Being an assertive communicator has three main requirements:
- being honest and straightforward, and using direct language to get your message across,
- being respectful of others' needs and feelings so that you create an open platform for communication, and
- using assertive body language and tone to match the style of the verbal messages you convey.

# BEING HONEST AND STRAIGHTFORWARD

**Being honest and straightforward**

The cornerstone of communicating assertively is being honest and straightforward. To do this, you need to be aware of your own emotions. And you need to express your feelings and needs directly, using precise language.

The problem with being indirect or hinting is that it involves relying on your listener to guess what you're really trying to say. A more direct request conveys the speaker's real meaning clearly.

**Question**

Take the example of asking for a raise.

How do you think you should frame your statement or question to convey your meaning directly?

**Options:**

1. "With the new responsibilities I've taken on, I'd like to ask for a raise."

2. "I'm doing a lot more around here than I used to, don't you think?"

3. "Most employees who take on the responsibilities that I have are eligible for a raise."

4. "I deserve a raise."

**Answer:**

Option 1: This is the correct option. This statement clearly asserts your request and your reason for making it.

Option 2: This option is not very direct. It asks the other person's opinion rather than assertively expressing your own opinion. And it only hints you might be interested in a raise.

Option 3: This is a very indirect way to make a request. In fact, there's no request in the statement at all – just a hint.

Option 4: This option may seem direct, but it states your opinion as fact without owning it as your perspective. This is actually an indirect way to communicate.

Three main guidelines can help you communicate in a way that's straightforward and honest. These are using "I" statements to take ownership of your opinions, using accurate descriptions instead of exaggerations or judgments, and using direct language to convey meaning.

It's a good habit always to express your opinions using "I" statements – for example, starting with "I think..." or "I believe..." In this way, you take ownership of your ideas. You also avoid the aggressive tactic of stating your opinions as facts, and this shows respect for the opinions of others.

Consider a statement like "You've been ignoring my instructions." This may provoke a negative response – or result in no response at all from someone who feels under attack.

Simply preceding a statement with "I feel," "I get the impression," or "I am concerned" makes it clear that you're presenting your opinion, so it opens the way for the person you're addressing to respond with an explanation. For instance, "I feel that my instructions have been ignored" is a more assertive version of "You've ignored my instructions," which is an accusation.

However, it's important to realize that just because a statement begins with "I" doesn't mean it qualifies as a true "I" statement.

**Question**

Do you think "I feel that you don't spend enough time checking the quality of your reports" is a good example of an assertive "I" statement?

**Options:**

1. Yes
2. No

**Answer**

This "I" statement isn't a good example of an assertive statement that's honest or direct. Instead, it's like a disguised "you" statement. It's aggressive rather than assertive because it takes the form of an accusation instead of a true expression of the speaker's feelings.

True "I" statements honestly express how you feel about something. For instance, you may feel irritated, concerned, anxious, or frustrated.

**"You always interrupt me!"**

"You always interrupt me!" is an accusation. By changing it to use the "I" statement, you change it into an honest and direct expression of how you feel about being interrupted.

*Alternative "I" statement: "I would like to be able to finish my points without being interrupted."*

**"You make me so mad."**

"You make me so mad" reflects confusion and hostility. By rephrasing how you feel using the "I" statement, you express the honest anger that's present in the "you" statement, but you're less likely to create confusion and hostility.

*Alternative "I" statement: "I get angry when you don't get your reports done on time."*

**"If you don't hurry up with the reports, this project is going to fail."**

"If you don't hurry up with the reports, this project is going to fail" reflects pure anxiety. By using the "I" statement, you take ownership of the anxiety you feel, without exaggerating or blaming the other person. At the same time, you assertively demonstrate the seriousness of the situation.

*Alternative "I" statement: "I'm concerned that if the reports aren't complete by next week, the whole project will be threatened."*

As well as taking ownership of your words, you should be accurate. Judgmental or exaggerated language shows a lack of respect for the listener and rarely has any place in assertive dialog. For example, a statement like "You never lift a finger to help around the office" is unlikely to foster a constructive discussion. A less judgmental and exaggerated statement is "I feel you don't offer much help around the office." This encourages a rational response.

Many people are afraid of being assertive because they think that by speaking directly, they may come across as pushy or forward. This often leads to overly polite speech consisting of indirect requests and vague hints, which can be confusing.

To be an effective, assertive communicator, you need to watch out for vague or presumptuous statements, and be direct in your requests.

For example, avoid introducing your opinions using negative wording or questions like "Don't you think that..." Instead, say what you mean directly. A clear statement is more assertive than an indirect one.

Follow along as Darren and Sara, two project leaders, discuss new information relating to a contract with William, their manager.

**Darren:** I've just read the e-mail regarding the new schedule for the Tek Weekly job. The deadlines are tighter, and we still haven't advertised for new programmers!

**William:** You always blow things out of proportion, Darren. Things will be fine!

**Sara:** Why don't you offer the team another production bonus?

**William:** I just need everything to run smoothly.

**Darren:** A bonus isn't the issue, Sara. And things aren't likely to run smoothly, William, because there isn't enough time to complete the project with our current staff resources. Will you please advertise for new programmers as soon as possible?

Both Sara and William use indirect and unassertive language. William aggressively states that Darren "always blows things out of proportion," as if this is a fact. Darren responds defensively, which creates conflict between them. If William had used assertive language, he would have given Darren the space to express himself, instead of insulting him.

Sara makes a vague suggestion about how to get the work done on time in the form of a "Why don't you...?" question. Her indirect response to the problem frustrates Darren because it merely shifts the problem onto him. Sara should have made a direct request to William, her manager, for a bonus to act as motivation for a team that won't increase in size but must deliver more work on time.

William also phrases his wish for the project to run smoothly as "I just need..." This is really an indirect request, so it should've been followed by a spoken request or directive. The assumption that Darren will automatically act on William's need demonstrates his lack of respect for Darren.

**Question**

Consider this statement: "You fail at everything you try because of your bad attitude."

Which is the best assertive replacement for the statement?

**Options:**

1. "You fail at everything you try, and I feel you have a bad attitude."

2. "I think you fail at everything you try because of your bad attitude."

3. "Your bad attitude is the cause of your frequent failures."

4. "I believe you frequently fail at things you try and that your attitude is the cause."

5. "Haven't you noticed you fail more often when you have a negative attitude?"

**Answer:**

## Interpersonal Communication

Option 1: This option is incorrect. The first part of this statement is exaggerated. In the second part, the speaker has used "I" but it's really a disguised "you" statement, so the speaker hasn't fully taken ownership of the opinion.

Option 2: This is an incorrect option. In this statement, the speaker has taken ownership of the opinions by using "I." However, the statement is exaggerated and judgmental.

Option 3: This is an incorrect option. This statement gives an opinion as fact. The speaker hasn't used "I" to take ownership of the opinions, and the statement is judgmental.

Option 4: This is the correct option. This statement takes ownership of the opinions presented through the use of "I" and changes the exaggeration to something more direct and accurate.

Option 5: This option is incorrect. This statement is indirect, which obscures the speaker's opinion. It's not fully clear what the speaker intends to communicate with this statement. It also presents the connection between failure and attitude as if it was fact, rather than opinion.

# BEING RESPECTFUL OF OTHERS

**Being respectful of others**

As an assertive communicator, it's vital to demonstrate respect for others' needs and feelings. If you fail to do this, others will be less receptive to what you say and may lose respect for you.

Three practical tips help you demonstrate respect for others when you communicate:
- start with a positive to make communication less confrontational,
- show respect for the other person's position by acknowledging what it means to that,
- person present your opinion neutrally and without being abrasive.

**Start with a positive**

Even if you disagree with what the other person has said, find something you can agree on – a positive or something you like about the other's opinion – and start by mentioning that.

**Show respect for the other person's position**

You should demonstrate respect for another person's point of view, even if you don't share it. Belittling someone else's contributions is an aggressive approach that can make others less receptive to what you have to say. Besides, the other person may have a valuable perspective on the issue that you hadn't considered.

**Present your opinion neutrally**

After recognizing the other person's viewpoint, you should present yours as one possibility of many, without being abrasive. In this way, your opinion remains neutral.

Respecting the needs and feelings of others sometimes means accepting their refusal of a request or suggestion you made. A truly respectful communicator will always give people the right to pass on decisions, to disagree, or to say "no."

Consider a statement like "Your proposal still needs a lot of work." A more respectful version, which is far more likely to have a constructive effect, is "I think this proposal could do with some improvements. Can we go over it together?"

**Question**

Which statements demonstrate respect for the needs and feelings of the listener?

**Options:**

1. "That's ridiculous. Everyone knows that riding a bicycle to work is the environmentally friendly choice."

2. "I agree that cars aren't environmentally friendly, but I believe that scooters also produce a fair amount of pollution."

3. "We both agree that environmentally friendly transportation is the way to go, but I don't see myself riding a scooter."

4. "I believe we should be more environmentally aware, but riding a scooter to work every day is just crazy."

5. "I'm glad you've found your new scooter to be a great fuel-saving option! Unfortunately, it wouldn't work well for me because I take my son to daycare each day."

**Answer:**

Option 1: This option is incorrect. This statement presents opinion as fact – and in an abrasive manner. This leaves the other person little room to respond in a nonconfrontational manner.

Option 2: This is a correct option. This statement attempts to find common ground with the other person and takes ownership of the opinion given. This gives room for different opinions and demonstrates respect for the listener.

Option 3: This option is correct. This statement opens with a positive in the form of common ground between the speaker and listener. It also takes ownership of the opinion given, allows room for different opinions, and shows respect for the listener.

Option 4: This is an incorrect option. This statement attempts to find common ground with the other person, but it abrasively presents opinion as fact.

Option 5: This is a correct option. Not only does this statement start with a positive, but it also acknowledges the other person's perspective and experience.

# USING ASSERTIVE BODY LANGUAGE AND TONE

**Using assertive body language and tone**

You need to make certain that your body language matches the assertiveness of your words, if you want to come across as assertive to your listener. If you use unassertive body language, you will lessen the impact of what you're saying, or send potentially confusing signals to others.

Just like words, different postures, facial expressions, and vocal characteristics are associated with each of the three types of behaviors: passive, assertive, or aggressive.

**Passive**

Examples of passive body language include slumped posture with stooped shoulders, nervous shifting or hand gestures, shrugs, blinking, a nervous smile, and biting the lower lip. Passive vocal behaviors include speaking softly, hesitating, nervously laughing, and raising the voice at the end of sentences so that they sound like questions.

**Assertive**

Assertive body language includes an upright yet relaxed posture, a comfortable demeanor, calm hand gestures, very little blinking, and facial expressions that match the intent of the message. Assertive vocal behavior includes speaking in a calm and resonant voice, laughing and smiling appropriately, and using a neutral pitch.

**Aggressive**

Aggressive body language includes rigid posture with shoulders thrown back, jerky or tense demeanor, choppy hand gestures, clenched jaw, and a furrowed brow with an angry glare, grimace, or sarcastic smile. People who are communicating in an aggressive way may also sit with their feet up or their hands behind their heads. Vocally, signs of aggression include speaking in a tone that's harsh, loud, dictatorial, or sarcastic, speaking in a clipped manner, and sometimes using sarcastic laughter.

If you're aware of your own emotional triggers, you can make sure that you avoid behavior that's either aggressive or too passive. It's vital to recognize and control your emotions when you communicate with others. You can judge your own behavior and style of communication by watching your body language and others' reactions to you. If other people react angrily or clam up, you are probably acting aggressively. And if you find that your views are being overlooked, it's likely you're being too passive.

**Case Study: Question 1 of 3**

**Scenario**

For your convenience, the case study is repeated with each question.

Follow along as Alex, an online advertiser, and Lucy, a marketing manager for a technology e-zine, discuss a new campaign.

**Alex:** I've been going over the details of your company's contract, and frankly, it isn't good enough.

*Alex is angry and is making chopping, jerky gestures with his hands.*

**Lucy:** I beg your pardon, Alex? I thought we had closure on this a week ago. What's the problem?

*Lucy has her head slightly off to one side, and a serious expression on her face. She sounds alarmed.*

**Alex:** It's ridiculous! I've just compared the space rates for a couple of other IT e-zines and I'm getting ripped off here!

*Alex is angry, tense, and stern. His jaw is clenched.*

**Lucy:** Yes, our rates are higher, but they're appropriate considering our readership. I think it's too late to bring up such concerns, but perhaps we can sort something out.

*Lucy has her head off to one side, her hand up to her face, and a serious expression.*

**Alex:** You're emptying my bank account with a single mouse click! This makes me livid!

*Alex is standing rigid with his jaw clenched and a glare on his face. His voice conveys anger.*

**Lucy:** In my opinion, we offer competitive rates, but if you break down the costs and point out problem areas, we may be able to offer you a discount on any further runs.

*Lucy has her head off to one side, her hand up to her face, and a serious expression.*

**Alex:** Alright, Lucy. I'll put a breakdown together.

Alex looks and sounds more relaxed. His arms are by his sides.

### Question

Which is the first honest and straightforward statement in the conversation between Alex and Lucy? Options:

1. "I've been going over the details of your company's contract, and frankly, it isn't good enough."
2. "I thought we had closure on this a week ago."
3. "It's ridiculous!"
4. "You're emptying my bank account!"
5. "In my opinion, we offer competitive rates."

**Answer:**

Option 1: This option is incorrect. In this sentence, Alex states his opinion as fact, rather than using a straightforward "I" statement.

Option 2: This is the correct option. Lucy expresses her opinion and doesn't exaggerate or resort to judgment.

Option 3: This is an incorrect option. This is a judgmental opinion that Alex states as fact.

Option 4: This option is incorrect. Alex states his opinion as fact and resorts to exaggeration to make a point.

Option 5: This option is incorrect. While this is an honest and straightforward statement, it's not the first such statement in the dialog.

**Case Study: Question 2 of 3**

Which statements demonstrate respect for the other person's feelings and positions?

**Options:**

1. "I've been going over the details of your company's contract, and frankly, it isn't good enough."
2. "Yes, our rates are higher, but they're appropriate considering our readership."
3. "You're emptying my bank account with a single mouse click!"

4. "In my opinion, we offer competitive rates, but if you break down the costs and point out problem areas, we may be able to offer you a discount on any further runs."

**Answer:**

Option 1: This is an incorrect option. Alex delivers this statement abrasively, with no concern for Lucy's position.

Option 2: This is a correct option. Although Lucy disagrees with Alex, she starts with a positive stance and then introduces her conflicting opinion.

Option 3: This option is incorrect. This aggressive statement from Alex is an exaggerated accusation that left no room for disagreement.

Option 4: This option is correct. Lucy shows respect for Alex's position despite her differing opinion. She also presents her opinion without being abrasive.

**Case Study: Question 3 of 3**

Was Alex's body language assertive?

**Options:**

1. Yes, it was assertive
2. No, it was aggressive
3. No, it was passive

**Answer:**

Option 1: This is an incorrect option. Alex clearly displayed aggressive body language. Assertive body language includes an erect but relaxed posture, straight shoulders, relaxed hands and hand gestures, a genuine smile where appropriate, and a calm voice.

Option 2: This is the correct option. Alex displayed aggressive body language. His posture was rigid and his body was tense. He made jerky and sudden hand gestures, grimaced angrily, and spoke in a harsh and angry tone of voice.

Option 3: This is an incorrect option. Alex clearly displayed aggressive body language. Passive body language can include a slumped posture with stooped shoulders; nervousness; quick hand gestures; a nervous or guilty smile; and a soft, high pitched voice, often with questioning inflections.

# SECTION 3 - COMMUNICATING ASSERTIVELY

## SECTION 3 - Communicating Assertively

To incrementally escalate the power of your assertiveness if you fail to get an appropriate response, you should start by repeating your request. Then rephrase it as a directive, add emotion, and finally, outline a consequence that will occur if the listener still fails to respond.

# ESCALATING ASSERTIVENESS

**Escalating assertiveness**

Being assertive at work is advantageous in many ways. It is never necessary to become aggressive to express your opinion or to get what you want. When communicating assertively, you speak honestly and in a straightforward manner, show respect for the person you're interacting with, and use assertive body language.

But what do you do if you've met all the requirements for an assertive communication and your message still doesn't get through to the other person? Even if you're being assertive, someone may fail to respond. What then? If someone isn't responding to you in a desired way, and you really need them to, there are four steps you can follow to incrementally escalate the power of your assertiveness:

1. repeat what you have said to ensure you've been understood,

2. reframe your request or statement as a directive to make it clear that it's imperative for the listener to respond in the way you've requested,

## Interpersonal Communication

3. add emotion to what you say so that the listener knows you're serious, and

4. add consequences if the listener still doesn't respond in the way you've requested.

### 1. Repeat

By repeating what you've said assertively, you give the other person a second chance to respond in an appropriate way. This person may not have heard you the first time or may not have been listening fully. Sometimes it helps to emphasize certain words.

### 2. Reframe as a directive

In some cases, a colleague or someone you manage at work may ignore an assertive request. You should then consider rephrasing your request or statement so that it sounds more like a command. This gives more power to your request. For example, you could change a request like "Could you tell me where the meeting room is?" to a directive like "Please tell me where the meeting room is." Because this is more direct, it's more likely to elicit a response.

### 3. Add emotion

If someone doesn't respond to a directive, you should then include emotion in your statements, if appropriate. For example, you could say "I'm getting worried because you're not answering me. Please can you tell me what you think of my idea?" Colleagues may not be used to emotions being expressed, so this may encourage them to give the appropriate response – and possibly to add an apology for not responding sooner. If an apology follows, it's appropriate for you to thank the person.

### 4. Add consequences

A consequence is not a threat – it is a statement of what will happen if the person does not respond. For example "If you do not get me the data, it will delay production and I'll have to report this to the line manager" is a valid response to someone who fails to submit information you need to do your job. Chances are, you will not reach this step in the escalation process because one of the earlier steps will prompt a response. The consequence you outline should be plausible to ensure that it's taken seriously. You should also be prepared to implement the consequence if the other person still doesn't respond.

You should make sure you use the steps only when appropriate and only in sequence. For example, it's only appropriate to issue a directive if a person has already failed to respond to a request. If you use a directive when you don't need to, a colleague may take offense and your behavior may be seen as pushy.

It's appropriate to outline a consequence only if you've already attempted the first three steps. When you add a consequence, you still give the other person a chance to respond in the appropriate way. But if you actually implement a consequence without stating it in advance, it can come across as aggressive and unfair – and may alienate the listener.

Question

You're in a meeting with a team member about how to make improvements to office communications. You have an idea to propose. You say "I was thinking – could we develop a notice board that is updated everyday?"

Your colleague doesn't respond. Sequence the examples of statements in order of increasing power of assertiveness.

**Options:**

## Interpersonal Communication

A. "Could we develop a notice board that is updated everyday?"

B. "Please tell me what you think of my idea about a notice board."

C. "I'm getting irritated that you're not responding. Please tell me what you think of my idea about a notice board."

D. "It's important that all ideas are acknowledged in a planning meeting. If you don't respond and tell me what you think of the idea of a notice board, we'll need to end this meeting."

**Answer**

"Could we develop a notice board that is updated everyday?" is ranked the first step. If your colleague doesn't respond at first, you should repeat what you originally said. Your colleague might not have heard what you said.

"Please tell me what you think of my idea about a notice board." is ranked the second step. If your colleague ignores your repetition and still fails to respond to your request, you can rephrase it as an imperative or a directive to encourage a response.

"I'm getting irritated that you're not responding. Please tell me what you think of my idea about a notice board." is ranked the third step. People don't often express emotion in requests. By doing this, you increase the power of your assertiveness and encourage a response. You should do this after you've tried rephrasing your request as a directive.

"It's important that all ideas are acknowledged in a planning meeting. If you don't respond and tell me what you think of the idea of a notice board, we'll need to end this meeting." is ranked the fourth step. You should outline a consequence of your colleague still failing to respond only after you've tried the first three steps. This adds a lot more power to your request and is likely to make your colleague respond.

# CHAPTER 5 - BEING APPROACHABLE

**CHAPTER 5 - Being Approachable**

# SECTION 1 - THE IMPORTANCE OF APPROACHABILITY

**SECTION 1 - The Importance of Approachability**

Being approachable is essential for effective communication. Although there are many aspects to approachability, some of the central ones are reaching out, being available, and helping others to feel confident, comfortable, and understood.

Being approachable brings many benefits. It builds trust and enhances relationships with others. It also ensures that more information is shared and that you receive more feedback. If you are approachable, more opportunities become available to you, and you are better able to further the success of your organization.

# BEING APPROACHABLE

**Being approachable**
Being approachable is one of the most important attributes of successful communicators. But what is approachability? And how do you become more approachable? The specific characteristics of approachability are varied and complex. However, you can still identify them and learn how to use them.

**Aspects central to approachability**
You can make yourself more approachable in many different ways, and you probably already know what some of these are. The foundation for approachability lies in three key aspects: reaching out to people, making yourself available to them, and helping people feel confident, comfortable, and understood when they're talking to you.

**Reaching out**
Reaching out is about being proactive in initiating contact. By approaching people, you actively show that you welcome new relationships and value the people you already know. This in turn makes it easier for people to approach you.

## Making yourself available

By making yourself available, you ensure you are physically and personally available to others. It becomes easy for others to contact you and to speak to you. To help others approach you, you need to be seen – so keep your door open and ensure that you sit where others can see you. You also need to be easy to contact by phone and e-mail. It's important to give people explicit permission to approach you by assuring them that they are welcome to contact you or talk with you.

## Making people feel confident, comfortable, and understood

Once you have made yourself available, or have initiated contact yourself, you need to continue to be approachable. If you remain open and attentive, and you put people at ease, they will feel confident, comfortable, and understood. This encourages people to approach you again.

# BENEFITS OF APPROACHABILITY

**Benefits of approachability**

Scott, the manager of a small trucking company, is often uncomfortable around others and spends most of his time in his office with the door closed. He is brusque when talking with colleagues and hardly ever uses their suggestions. He habitually blames others for problems that they bring to his attention and accuses them of incompetence.

The result is that many people who work at the company don't trust Scott very much and don't approach him when they have problems or queries. A few drivers notice that some people are overloading their trucks to save time on bulk contract work. Despite this being dangerous and illegal, no one has the courage to inform Scott.

The practice continues until an overloaded truck has an accident. The truck is damaged and the company is faced with a large fine. How could Scott's situation have been avoided?

There are many advantages to being more approachable. If you are approachable, people tend to trust you more and share more with you, so you're more likely to receive critical information and feedback. You gain more opportunities as you expand your social network and improve relationships at work. This in turn can generate more business for your company.

**Trust and sharing**

The more approachable you are, the more permission you give people to share their thoughts and feelings with you. When people feel safe and welcome, they develop trust toward you. Trust and rapport develop over time and depend on a personal connection that can be established if you are approachable.

With trust, you build better relationships and learn more about others' roles and perspectives in the organization. For example, if people trust you enough to share how they feel about a new process or procedure, you'll better understand how it affects employees beyond your immediate circle.

**Critical information and feedback**

If you welcome feedback, others will be willing to give it. You gain helpful – perhaps crucial – information through feedback. Negative feedback is more difficult to give than positive feedback, but the easier you are to approach, the more honest feedback from others will be. By being curious about how what you do affects others, you become more open.

For example, if you are an engineer and you make a mistake in your calculations, your subordinates should feel free to approach you and notify you of your error. If they are unable to do that, the results could be devastating.

### Opportunities

You gain more opportunities when you are approachable. By reaching out, you get to know people and, as a result, you learn what they have to offer you. So the wider your social network, the more opportunities you come across.

If you're approachable, people you know feel comfortable mentioning new possibilities. It's also important to be physically available if people are to offer you new prospects. For example, you might find out about a new job opportunity while chatting to a chance acquaintance at a friend's party.

### Improved relationships

If you are approachable, you'll enjoy improved relationships. This can generate a more relaxed and cooperative work culture. When colleagues trust one another and communicate well, interactions are more satisfying and enjoyable for everyone involved.

People feel more comfortable and heard, which improves the work environment and enables teams to meet their communication goals. In short, approachability makes it easier for you and your colleagues to work together as a team.

For example, making yourself available to attend planning meetings will give you opportunities to connect with your colleagues on both an interpersonal and a professional level, and will potentially enhance your relationships with them.

### More business

By being approachable, you may win more business for your company. Customers feel more comfortable and confident about buying from you or asking for your assistance. Customers base many of their purchasing decisions on the people they deal with, rather than on brands and products. They develop loyalty and trust toward people, not companies.

The more approachable you are, the better the response is likely to be from customers and others who you interact with on behalf of your company. For example, a customer is thinking about making a purchase. Because you are approachable, a relationship is established. This encourages the customer to trust you and your product, and can result in long-term customer loyalty.

How approachable do you think you are? How can you assess this quality in yourself?

Approachability can be measured in degrees or using an approachability index. Typically, people aren't either totally approachable or totally unapproachable. They may be quite approachable in some contexts and less so in others. Finding the strengths and weaknesses in your own approachability can help you to develop it further.

Some useful questions you can ask yourself when gauging your own approachability are "How often do others come to me to discuss issues?" "How often do they offer feedback, and how often is that feedback negative?" "Are people comfortable enough to disagree with me?" Other useful questions include "How do I typically deal with conflict?" "Do I tend to talk more than I listen?" "Am I curious about what others have to say?"

**Question**

When others find it easy to come to you with constructive criticism and for advice, it's a good sign that you have a high degree of approachability.

How easy do you think others find it to approach you to offer constructive criticism?

**Options:**

1. Usually easy
2. Sometimes easy
3. Hardly ever easy

**Answer:**

Option 1: You already have some of the skills you need to be approachable. How can you enhance your existing skills and develop new ones? Do you actively seek out others to communicate with?

Option 2: The fact that others sometimes feel comfortable offering you constructive criticism is a good indication you're already somewhat approachable. If you become hard to approach in particular situations, how can you make yourself more approachable in these situations?

Option 3: You need to work on some aspects of your approachability. Which aspects do you think may need attention? And what negative signals might you be giving out that make it hard for others to offer constructive criticism?

**Question**

Approachability can always be improved. What benefits are you likely to realize from enhancing your approachability?

**Options:**

1. Others will enjoy working with you more
2. You'll be more successful at furthering the interests of your company
3. You'll get to know more people, which can increase the number of opportunities that come your way

4. People will be more willing to share information with you

5. You won't be criticized as often

6. You'll be less distracted by other people's concerns and better able to focus on your own work

**Answer:**

Option 1: This option is correct. Being approachable builds rapport, and others feel more comfortable and confident around you. This makes working with you more enjoyable.

Option 2: This is a correct option. Being approachable enables you to interact with colleagues and customers more effectively, achieving mutual satisfaction and trust. This in turn gives you more influence to win business advantages for your company.

Option 3: This option is correct. When you're approachable, more opportunities may come your way because you enlarge your social network and enhance your communication with others. The result is that you're more likely to learn of opportunities, which gives you better chances of getting what you want.

Option 4: This option is correct. When people feel comfortable and confident about approaching you, they feel safe sharing information and ideas with you.

Option 5: This option is incorrect. Being approachable enables others to feel confident enough to offer you criticism when it's warranted.

Option 6: This option is incorrect. Being approachable requires you to be present for others. This requires a real investment of your time and energy in considering the needs of others, being available, and listening.

# SECTION 2 - REACHING OUT TO OTHERS, AND INVITING OTHERS IN

**SECTION 2 - Reaching Out to Others, and Inviting Others In**

To be approachable, you initiate contact by reaching out to people or by conveying to others that you want to be approached. You maintain approachability by being receptive to people during conversations with them. Outreach techniques you can use to initiate contact include starting up conversations – both with people you know and with strangers, seeking opportunities to encounter people, offering to help, and learning more about others and their interests.

To show others that you are available, you need to be physically available, rather than shut away in an office or focused on your computer. Additionally, you need to stay in touch with people and be easy to contact. In social situations, you need to show that the doors of communication are figuratively open by having open body language and a friendly demeanor.

# APPROACHABILITY DOMAINS

**Approachability domains**

It's easy to grasp the importance of being approachable. But how exactly do you go about becoming approachable? Three domains contribute to this. They are outreach, availability, and reception. All three domains are necessary for maximizing your approachability.

**Outreach**

Outreach, or "outbound approachability," refers to how you proactively expand the contacts you have. It involves initiating communication encounters – being bold and friendly. There are many ways to break the ice and give people the opportunity to connect with you. The more ways you reach out, the more approachable you become.

**Availability**

Availability, or "inbound approachability," involves making yourself available to others. If you convey availability, people feel more comfortable approaching you. To do this, you need to avoid being aloof, mysterious, or creating a sense of "mystique" because this works against your approachability.

**Reception**

Reception involves putting people at ease while you speak to them. It's important to foster trust and comfort in others when you're communicating with them. They'll remember this next time they approach you.

When talking with others, it's important that you don't continue with other tasks and that you avoid interruptions to the conversation. Your behavior and body language need to be welcoming. If you listen authentically and respond to what people are saying with warmth and acceptance, you make yourself available to others on a personal level.

The three domains of approachability fit intuitively together in any given communication event. First, you need a way to initiate communication. You do this through outreach behaviors or by making yourself available and inviting contact from others. Once contact has been initiated, either by you or by someone else, you sustain it by being receptive.

**Question**

Match each domain of approachability to its key function. Not all functions will be used.

**Options:**

A. Outreach
B. Availability
C. Reception

**Targets:**

1. To make contacts
2. To invite or attract contacts
3. To maintain your contacts

4. To make your contacts more available

**Answer**

You reach out to people in order to make contact with them. This enables you to initiate communication.

You invite others to make contact with you by showing you're available. This encourages them to initiate communication with you.

You maintain contact with others by being receptive to them and what they have to say. People will remember your demeanor next time they consider communicating with you. Positive, receptive encounters enhance your approachability and help you maintain stronger relationships with contacts.

Making your contacts more available doesn't relate to your approachability. While your contacts may want to improve their own availability, you can't do anything to directly influence the availability of others.

# CLOSED DOORS

**Closed doors**

Outreach and availability are all about making contact to facilitate communication and convey approachability. However, substantial barriers can make you appear less open to others and so "close the door" on communication. The closed door may be literal or figurative, but either way, it reduces the likelihood that contact will be initiated.

**Literal closed doors**

Literal closed doors are physical barriers that have a psychological effect. If you are physically isolated from others by a closed office door, for instance, you won't seem available to be approached.

While many people view an office with a door as a symbol of status within an organization, having one can make you less approachable and cocoon you from your coworkers. The less you interact with others, the more closed off you become. Cubicle walls can also isolate you and make you unapproachable, as can wearing headphones and listening to music while working.

**Figurative closed doors**

You may give off signals that indicate you're not available – that your figurative door is closed. If you are engrossed in reading, your arms are folded, or you avoid eye-contact, people can sometimes understand this to mean that you want to keep your distance and don't want to talk with them. You are effectively withholding permission for other people to approach you, and they respond accordingly.

People are often reticent about making contact with others. They may fear that they're imposing on you, and may not be sure they're welcome to contact you. Or, they may feel shy or anxious about approaching you. So to be approachable, you need to show you're not only physically available, but also available on a personal level – your doors are figuratively open.

**Question**

Which examples illustrate barriers to approachability?

**Options:**

1. Taking detailed notes, which requires continuous typing on your laptop, during a meeting
2. Habitually taking your coffee and lunch breaks in a quiet area where nobody else goes
3. Keeping your arms folded in social situations
4. Keeping your office door shut
5. Listening, rather than talking, in social situations
6. Sitting with people you don't know

**Answer:**

Option 1: This option is correct. By focusing your attention on your laptop, you make it hard for others to catch your eye or include you in a discussion. This behavior is a barrier to approachability because it implies you aren't giving people permission to approach you.

Option 2: This option is correct. Choosing a secluded place for your breaks can isolate you and signal to others you want to be alone, which can create a barrier to approachability.

Option 3: This option is correct. Keeping your arms folded can prevent others from approaching you because it forms a barrier between yourself and others. Some people may read this as a desire to be left alone.

Option 4: This option is correct. By keeping your office door closed, you put a physical barrier between yourself and others, which they may hesitate to cross. This makes you hard to approach.

Option 5: This option is incorrect. Listening rather than talking isn't a barrier to approachability. It enhances your approachability because it gives others permission to speak to you.

Option 6: This option is incorrect. By sitting with people you don't know, you give them the opportunity to make contact with you.

# OUTREACH TECHNIQUES

**Outreach techniques**

If you want to become more approachable, one important behavior to work on is proactively reaching out to others. There are several techniques you can use to reach out to people and initiate contact with them. One of the best ways to do this is to start talking with people. It's particularly useful to talk to new people, who have yet to feel comfortable with you. By starting conversations, you break the ice and establish contact.

**Talk to people**

Talking to people doesn't simply mean starting up a conversation – it also includes actively seeking out people to talk to. If you work in an isolated office environment, it can be difficult to talk with your colleagues. In this case, you need to make more of an effort to get in contact with others.

An effective way to do this is to walk through your office. You can try taking different routes through the building each day, and having coffee on another floor or in another area every now and then. You could also ensure that you eat lunch in the breakroom at least once a week and, instead of sending an e-mail, visit colleagues when you have work-related queries. You not only get to make contact but also find better solutions by discussing issues with the individuals involved.

**Talk to new people**

Just as you need to approach the people you know, you also need to reach out to those you don't know and make them feel welcome. Ask new people for their names and introduce yourself to them whenever possible. Greet and smile at people. Sit next to people you don't know at meetings and during coffee breaks, and start up conversations. If someone seems shy in a group context, try to connect with the person when there are fewer people around. Simply knowing and using people's names, or greeting and smiling at them, can be an effective way of reaching out.

**Start conversations**

Simply greeting people goes a long way toward making yourself approachable to them, but to be truly approachable, you also need to start up conversations. Stay to chat after meetings. Walk up to groups and individuals at events. Wearing a name tag can be helpful when you are at a conference or training workshop and have lots of interactions with new people.

If you are in a group situation, make sure that everyone is involved in the conversation. Try to ask questions, listen to the answers you receive, and get to know people.

**Question**

How often do you start up conversations with people you don't know?

**Options:**

1. Often
2. Occasionally
3. Rarely

**Answer**

Option 1: You've likely already developed many of the skills you need to reach out. Are there any situations in which you could do more? How can you improve the ways in which you reach out to new people? Do you find you tend to talk more than you listen in these situations?

Option 2: You probably need to practice reaching out more often. Perhaps start with the steps you find easy and gradually increase the ways in which you make contact with new people.

Option 3: While reaching out can seem difficult to begin with, the more you practice, the easier and more enjoyable it becomes. Which ways of reaching out would be comfortable for you? How can you find ways of reaching out while still feeling safe?

If you find it difficult to reach out to others, one of the least stressful ways to do so is to offer to help someone complete a task. This sets you at ease and makes it possible to get to know people by working together toward a common goal. This can be as simple as volunteering for kitchen duty at a workshop or helping someone carry things.

Even if you find it easy to reach out to people, offering to help is one of the best outreach techniques to use in a work context. Spend some of your time doing things for other people, regardless of the nature of the tasks. Offer your skills, such as computer know-how, when they are needed.

## Interpersonal Communication

When you have conversations with people, it's important to be prepared to ask meaningful questions and give meaningful information in return.

If you already have a good idea of what people would enjoy talking about, it's easier to start up a conversation with them. Colleagues will also find conversations with you more significant and interesting if you keep informed about issues that matter to them. This helps you to approach colleagues with meaningful information and questions about their work or, in some cases, personal matters.

Appropriate personal information that you can use to reach out to people includes their birthdays and anniversaries. If you are aware of other people's work concerns and ambitions, you can raise them as topics in discussions.

**Question**

What kinds of activities can help you to reach out to people?

**Options:**

1. Learning more about what individuals do at work
2. Offering to help others with a software problem
3. Chatting with people you already know during your breaks
4. Introducing people to one another if they haven't met before
5. Responding promptly to e-mails
6. Sticking with a predictable route through your workplace each day

**Answer:**

Option 1: This option is correct. If you learn more about people's work, you're then more informed about them. This ensures that you're better prepared for meaningful conversations with them.

Option 2: This option is correct. Offering to help people with their work can be a very good way of starting conversations and reaching out.

Option 3: This option is correct. Reaching out to people is a continuous process of getting to know them and setting them at ease, so chatting to people you know is a good way of reaching out.

Option 4: This option is correct. Introductions are an important method of reaching out and learning people's names. By introducing people to one another, you include people and help them feel comfortable.

Option 5: This option is incorrect. Although responding promptly to e-mails may indicate to people you're available and willing to communicate, it doesn't help you to reach out and initiate contact in the first place.

Option 6: This option is incorrect. Taking a different route to your desk each day is more likely to bring you into contact with new people, as well as people you already know, giving you the opportunity to reach out to more people.

**Making it easier to reach out**

Communication experts recommend you start with small steps in safe settings. Perhaps you could set yourself goals, such as to reach out to two new people a week, or to find out more about two of the people you already know at work. With practice, reaching out does get easier. Many people feel shy and uncomfortable in social settings, so perhaps you could share your discomfort with another shy person.

Encourage yourself by focusing on your successes and reminding yourself of your abilities. Some people do well with affirmations. For instance, you could choose to say to yourself that you're a good listener or that your insights are valuable. However you choose to go about it, positive self-talk can bolster your courage when you need to speak up.

# AVAILABILITY TECHNIQUES

**Availability techniques**
You can use several methods to show others that you are willing to be approached. These can be categorized into two main techniques: staying in touch and keeping an open door.

**Staying in touch**
If other people can't reach you, you are not available to be approached. So you need to keep in touch with your network and your contacts. People may need to contact you by e-mail or by phone, so it's important to make sure that people know your contact details. Try to keep business cards readily available, and make sure that people know they are welcome to get in touch with you.

If someone tries to contact you, you need to show that you take this person seriously and that you really are approachable. So you should respond to e-mails and phone calls promptly. Check your messages regularly to see whether anyone has tried to contact you. And if someone has left a message for you, try to respond promptly – generally, within a maximum of about 14 hours.

### Keeping an open door

Keeping an open door means ensuring that you remove barriers between yourself and other people. You need to be physically present if possible so that others can approach you – not separated from them by doors or other barriers. You also need to convey that you welcome being approached. People generally look for visual cues to see if they are welcome to approach you.

Your body language has to be inviting if others are to feel comfortable about initiating contact. This means that you need to keep your arms uncrossed and avoid self-comfort gestures, such as holding things in front of your face or fiddling. It's helpful to smile at people, make eye contact, and generally position yourself for conversation.

Think about socializing at a group event – a conference reception, for instance. When you're deciding whether or not to approach someone, you look at that person's body language. Someone who doesn't want to be approached may signal this in a variety of ways. Sometimes people cross their arms because they are cold, but crossed arms can also indicate shyness, insecurity, or depression. So when you cross your arms, people often assume that you want to be left alone.

Similarly, people who hide part of their faces behind objects – their hands, papers, or even coffee mugs – may be signaling withdrawal and a need to distance themselves from others. Fidgeting can send out the same message, or it can signal boredom and a lack of interest in other people. So if you want others to feel comfortable approaching you, you should avoid these gestures.

When in group situations, you show others that you are available through appropriate eye contact, smiling, and using open body language.

Make eye contact by scanning your environment and briefly meeting people's eyes. Be careful not to stare at people, but do show that you are aware of them. When you meet people's eyes, smiling a little shows that you are friendly. Try to avoid staring out of the window or at the floor. You need to show interest in people by looking at them.

Smiling puts people at ease, shows that you are having fun, and demonstrates friendliness. Smile often when you catch people's eyes and during small talk. Have you ever had the feeling that someone's smile was phony? Smiles that involve only the mouth and not the eyes often appear insincere to others. Authentic smiles push up into the eyes and use more facial muscles than mouth-only smiles.

Be sure to smile with your whole face, including your eyes, which should have a soft, warm expression to show that you are interested in other people and well-disposed toward them.

**Question**

You've just walked into a conference breakroom. Who is the most approachable person in the room?

Tina's body language is inviting. John is speaking on a cell phone. Amrit has her arms crossed and her expression is serious. Taku is covering his face with his hand, as if in thought.

**Options:**
1. Tina
2. Amrit
3. Taku

## Interpersonal Communication

4. John

**Answer**

Option 1: Tina is demonstrating she's approachable. Her body language is inviting. She's making eye contact and smiling.

Option 2: Amrit's arms are crossed and she's not smiling, which makes her seem unenthusiastic about making contact.

Option 3: Taku is looking down and his hand is obscuring his face. This suggests he doesn't want to be approached.

Option 4: John seems busy because he's on his cell phone; he isn't inviting contact.

**Question**

Which actions signal that you can approach other people?

**Options:**

1. Orienting their desks to face outward in an open-plan office
2. Smiling
3. Introducing themselves to you
4. Looking at their companions and at you
5. Sitting upright but in a relaxed way
6. Looking intently at the artwork in the room

**Answer:**

Option 1: This option is correct. Positioning desks so they face outward makes people physically available to be approached.

Option 2: This option is correct. Smiling demonstrates friendliness and a willingness to start a conversation.

Option 3: This option is incorrect. By introducing themselves, people are actually reaching out to you, rather than signaling availability.

Option 4: This option is correct. By looking at others, people show they're willing to engage and are open to being approached.

Option 5: This option is correct. An upright but relaxed posture indicates that a person is available to be approached.

Option 6: This option is incorrect. By looking away from others and appearing absorbed in the artwork, a person signals unavailability.

# SECTION 3 - REACHING OUT TO OTHERS, AND INVITING OTHERS IN

**SECTION 3 - Reaching Out to Others, and Inviting Others In**

To be approachable, you initiate contact by reaching out to people or by conveying to others that you want to be approached. You maintain approachability by being receptive to people during conversations with them. Outreach techniques you can use to initiate contact include starting up conversations – both with people you know and with strangers, seeking opportunities to encounter people, offering to help, and learning more about others and their interests.

To show others that you are available, you need to be physically available, rather than shut away in an office or focused on your computer. Additionally, you need to stay in touch with people and be easy to contact. In social situations, you need to show that the doors of communication are figuratively open by having open body language and a friendly demeanor.

# APPROACHABILITY DOMAINS

**Approachability domains**

It's easy to grasp the importance of being approachable. But how exactly do you go about becoming approachable? Three domains contribute to this. They are outreach, availability, and reception. All three domains are necessary for maximizing your approachability.

**Outreach**

Outreach, or "outbound approachability," refers to how you proactively expand the contacts you have. It involves initiating communication encounters – being bold and friendly. There are many ways to break the ice and give people the opportunity to connect with you. The more ways you reach out, the more approachable you become.

**Availability**

Availability, or "inbound approachability," involves making yourself available to others. If you convey availability, people feel more comfortable approaching you. To do this, you need to avoid being aloof, mysterious, or creating a sense of "mystique" because this works against your approachability.

**Reception**

Reception involves putting people at ease while you speak to them. It's important to foster trust and comfort in others when you're communicating with them. They'll remember this next time they approach you. When talking with others, it's important that you don't continue with other tasks and that you avoid interruptions to the conversation.

Your behavior and body language need to be welcoming. If you listen authentically and respond to what people are saying with warmth and acceptance, you make yourself available to others on a personal level.

The three domains of approachability fit intuitively together in any given communication event. First, you need a way to initiate communication. You do this through outreach behaviors or by making yourself available and inviting contact from others. Once contact has been initiated, either by you or by someone else, you sustain it by being receptive.

Question

Match each domain of approachability to its key function. Not all functions will be used.

**Options:**

A. Outreach
B. Availability
C. Reception

**Targets:**

1. To make contacts
2. To invite or attract contacts
3. To maintain your contacts

4. To make your contacts more available

**Answer:**

You reach out to people in order to make contact with them. This enables you to initiate communication.

You invite others to make contact with you by showing you're available. This encourages them to initiate communication with you.

You maintain contact with others by being receptive to them and what they have to say. People will remember your demeanor next time they consider communicating with you. Positive, receptive encounters enhance your approachability and help you maintain stronger relationships with contacts.

Making your contacts more available doesn't relate to your approachability. While your contacts may want to improve their own availability, you can't do anything to directly influence the availability of others.

# CLOSED DOORS

**Closed doors**

Outreach and availability are all about making contact to facilitate communication and convey approachability. However, substantial barriers can make you appear less open to others and so "close the door" on communication. The closed door may be literal or figurative, but either way, it reduces the likelihood that contact will be initiated.

**Literal closed doors**

Literal closed doors are physical barriers that have a psychological effect. If you are physically isolated from others by a closed office door, for instance, you won't seem available to be approached.

While many people view an office with a door as a symbol of status within an organization, having one can make you less approachable and cocoon you from your coworkers. The less you interact with others, the more closed off you become. Cubicle walls can also isolate you and make you unapproachable, as can wearing headphones and listening to music while working.

**Figurative closed doors**

You may give off signals that indicate you're not available – that your figurative door is closed. If you are engrossed in reading, your arms are folded, or you avoid eye-contact, people can sometimes understand this to mean that you want to keep your distance and don't want to talk with them. You are effectively withholding permission for other people to approach you, and they respond accordingly.

People are often reticent about making contact with others. They may fear that they're imposing on you, and may not be sure they're welcome to contact you. Or, they may feel shy or anxious about approaching you. So to be approachable, you need to show you're not only physically available, but also available on a personal level – your doors are figuratively open.

**Question**

Which examples illustrate barriers to approachability?

**Options:**

1. Taking detailed notes, which requires continuous typing on your laptop, during a meeting

2. Habitually taking your coffee and lunch breaks in a quiet area where nobody else goes

3. Keeping your arms folded in social situations

4. Keeping your office door shut

5. Listening, rather than talking, in social situations

6. Sitting with people you don't know

**Answer:**

Option 1: This option is correct. By focusing your attention on your laptop, you make it hard for others to catch your eye or include you in a discussion. This behavior is a barrier to approachability because it implies you aren't giving people permission to approach you.

Option 2: This option is correct. Choosing a secluded place for your breaks can isolate you and signal to others you want to be alone, which can create a barrier to approachability.

Option 3: This option is correct. Keeping your arms folded can prevent others from approaching you because it forms a barrier between yourself and others. Some people may read this as a desire to be left alone.

Option 4: This option is correct. By keeping your office door closed, you put a physical barrier between yourself and others, which they may hesitate to cross. This makes you hard to approach.

Option 5: This option is incorrect. Listening rather than talking isn't a barrier to approachability. It enhances your approachability because it gives others permission to speak to you.

Option 6: This option is incorrect. By sitting with people you don't know, you give them the opportunity to make contact with you.

# OUTREACH TECHNIQUES

**Outreach techniques**

If you want to become more approachable, one important behavior to work on is proactively reaching out to others. There are several techniques you can use to reach out to people and initiate contact with them. One of the best ways to do this is to start talking with people. It's particularly useful to talk to new people, who have yet to feel comfortable with you. By starting conversations, you break the ice and establish contact.

**Talk to people**

Talking to people doesn't simply mean starting up a conversation – it also includes actively seeking out people to talk to. If you work in an isolated office environment, it can be difficult to talk with your colleagues. In this case, you need to make more of an effort to get in contact with others.

An effective way to do this is to walk through your office. You can try taking different routes through the building each day, and having coffee on another floor or in another area every now and then. You could also ensure that you eat lunch in the breakroom at least once a week and, instead of sending an e-mail, visit colleagues when you have work-related queries. You not only get to make contact but also find better solutions by discussing issues with the individuals involved.

**Talk to new people**

Just as you need to approach the people you know, you also need to reach out to those you don't know and make them feel welcome.

Ask new people for their names and introduce yourself to them whenever possible. Greet and smile at people. Sit next to people you don't know at meetings and during coffee breaks, and start up conversations. If someone seems shy in a group context, try to connect with the person when there are fewer people around. Simply knowing and using people's names, or greeting and smiling at them, can be an effective way of reaching out.

**Start conversations**

Simply greeting people goes a long way toward making yourself approachable to them, but to be truly approachable, you also need to start up conversations.

Stay to chat after meetings. Walk up to groups and individuals at events. Wearing a name tag can be helpful when you are at a conference or training workshop and have lots of interactions with new people. If you are in a group situation, make sure that everyone is involved in the conversation. Try to ask questions, listen to the answers you receive, and get to know people.

**Question**

How often do you start up conversations with people you don't know?

**Options:**

1. Often
2. Occasionally
3. Rarely

**Answer**

Option 1: You've likely already developed many of the skills you need to reach out. Are there any situations in which you could do more? How can you improve the ways in which you reach out to new people? Do you find you tend to talk more than you listen in these situations?

Option 2: You probably need to practice reaching out more often. Perhaps start with the steps you find easy and gradually increase the ways in which you make contact with new people.

Option 3: While reaching out can seem difficult to begin with, the more you practice, the easier and more enjoyable it becomes. Which ways of reaching out would be comfortable for you? How can you find ways of reaching out while still feeling safe?

If you find it difficult to reach out to others, one of the least stressful ways to do so is to offer to help someone complete a task. This sets you at ease and makes it possible to get to know people by working together toward a common goal. This can be as simple as volunteering for kitchen duty at a workshop or helping someone carry things.

Even if you find it easy to reach out to people, offering to help is one of the best outreach techniques to use in a work context. Spend some of your time doing things for other people, regardless of the nature of the tasks. Offer your skills, such as computer know-how, when they are needed.

## Interpersonal Communication

When you have conversations with people, it's important to be prepared to ask meaningful questions and give meaningful information in return.

If you already have a good idea of what people would enjoy talking about, it's easier to start up a conversation with them. Colleagues will also find conversations with you more significant and interesting if you keep informed about issues that matter to them. This helps you to approach colleagues with meaningful information and questions about their work or, in some cases, personal matters.

Appropriate personal information that you can use to reach out to people includes their birthdays and anniversaries. If you are aware of other people's work concerns and ambitions, you can raise them as topics in discussions.

**Question**

What kinds of activities can help you to reach out to people?

**Options:**

1. Learning more about what individuals do at work
2. Offering to help others with a software problem
3. Chatting with people you already know during your breaks
4. Introducing people to one another if they haven't met before
5. Responding promptly to e-mails
6. Sticking with a predictable route through your workplace each day

**Answer:**

Option 1: This option is correct. If you learn more about people's work, you're then more informed about them. This ensures that you're better prepared for meaningful conversations with them.

Option 2: This option is correct. Offering to help people with their work can be a very good way of starting conversations and reaching out.

Option 3: This option is correct. Reaching out to people is a continuous process of getting to know them and setting them at ease, so chatting to people you know is a good way of reaching out.

Option 4: This option is correct. Introductions are an important method of reaching out and learning people's names. By introducing people to one another, you include people and help them feel comfortable.

Option 5: This option is incorrect. Although responding promptly to e-mails may indicate to people you're available and willing to communicate, it doesn't help you to reach out and initiate contact in the first place.

Option 6: This option is incorrect. Taking a different route to your desk each day is more likely to bring you into contact with new people, as well as people you already know, giving you the opportunity to reach out to more people.

**Making it easier to reach out**

Communication experts recommend you start with small steps in safe settings. Perhaps you could set yourself goals, such as to reach out to two new people a week, or to find out more about two of the people you already know at work. With practice, reaching out does get easier. Many people feel shy and uncomfortable in social settings, so perhaps you could share your discomfort with another shy person.

Encourage yourself by focusing on your successes and reminding yourself of your abilities. Some people do well with affirmations. For instance, you could choose to say to yourself that you're a good listener or that your insights are valuable. However you choose to go about it, positive self-talk can bolster your courage when you need to speak up.

# AVAILABILITY TECHNIQUES

**Availability techniques**

You can use several methods to show others that you are willing to be approached. These can be categorized into two main techniques: staying in touch and keeping an open door.

**Staying in touch**

If other people can't reach you, you are not available to be approached. So you need to keep in touch with your network and your contacts.

People may need to contact you by e-mail or by phone, so it's important to make sure that people know your contact details. Try to keep business cards readily available, and make sure that people know they are welcome to get in touch with you.

If someone tries to contact you, you need to show that you take this person seriously and that you really are approachable. So you should respond to e-mails and phone calls promptly. Check your messages regularly to see whether anyone has tried to contact you. And if someone has left a message for you, try to respond promptly – generally, within a maximum of about 14 hours.

### Keeping an open door

Keeping an open door means ensuring that you remove barriers between yourself and other people. You need to be physically present if possible so that others can approach you – not separated from them by doors or other barriers.

You also need to convey that you welcome being approached. People generally look for visual cues to see if they are welcome to approach you.

Your body language has to be inviting if others are to feel comfortable about initiating contact. This means that you need to keep your arms uncrossed and avoid self-comfort gestures, such as holding things in front of your face or fiddling. It's helpful to smile at people, make eye contact, and generally position yourself for conversation.

Think about socializing at a group event – a conference reception, for instance. When you're deciding whether or not to approach someone, you look at that person's body language. Someone who doesn't want to be approached may signal this in a variety of ways. Sometimes people cross their arms because they are cold, but crossed arms can also indicate shyness, insecurity, or depression. So when you cross your arms, people often assume that you want to be left alone.

Similarly, people who hide part of their faces behind objects – their hands, papers, or even coffee mugs – may be signaling withdrawal and a need to distance themselves from others. Fidgeting can send out the same message, or it can signal boredom and a lack of interest in other people. So if you want others to feel comfortable approaching you, you should avoid these gestures.

When in group situations, you show others that you are available through appropriate eye contact, smiling, and using open body language.

Make eye contact by scanning your environment and briefly meeting people's eyes. Be careful not to stare at people, but do show that you are aware of them. When you meet people's eyes, smiling a little shows that you are friendly. Try to avoid staring out of the window or at the floor. You need to show interest in people by looking at them.

Smiling puts people at ease, shows that you are having fun, and demonstrates friendliness. Smile often when you catch people's eyes and during small talk. Have you ever had the feeling that someone's smile was phony? Smiles that involve only the mouth and not the eyes often appear insincere to others. Authentic smiles push up into the eyes and use more facial muscles than mouth-only smiles.

Be sure to smile with your whole face, including your eyes, which should have a soft, warm expression to show that you are interested in other people and well-disposed toward them.

You display open body language by sitting or standing fairly upright in a relaxed rather than rigid position, keeping your arms uncrossed, and orienting your face and body toward others. Always try to put yourself on the same level as others by sitting or standing in the same way as most people in the room. Sitting when others are standing, or standing when others are sitting, diminishes your approachability.

**Question**

## Interpersonal Communication

You've just walked into a conference breakroom. Who is the most approachable person in the room?

Tina's body language is inviting. John is speaking on a cell phone. Amrit has her arms crossed and her expression is serious. Taku is covering his face with his hand, as if in thought.

**Options:**
1. Tina
2. Amrit
3. Taku
4. John

**Answer:**

Option 1: Tina is demonstrating she's approachable. Her body language is inviting. She's making eye contact and smiling.

Option 2: Amrit's arms are crossed and she's not smiling, which makes her seem unenthusiastic about making contact.

Option 3: Taku is looking down and his hand is obscuring his face. This suggests he doesn't want to be approached.

Option 4: John seems busy because he's on his cell phone; he isn't inviting contact.

**Question**

Which actions signal that you can approach other people?

**Options:**
1. Orienting their desks to face outward in an open-plan office
2. Smiling
3. Introducing themselves to you
4. Looking at their companions and at you

5. Sitting upright but in a relaxed way

6. Looking intently at the artwork in the room

**Answer**

Option 1: This option is correct. Positioning desks so they face outward makes people physically available to be approached.

Option 2: This option is correct. Smiling demonstrates friendliness and a willingness to start a conversation.

Option 3: This option is incorrect. By introducing themselves, people are actually reaching out to you, rather than signaling availability.

Option 4: This option is correct. By looking at others, people show they're willing to engage and are open to being approached.

Option 5: This option is correct. An upright but relaxed posture indicates that a person is available to be approached.

Option 6: This option is incorrect. By looking away from others and appearing absorbed in the artwork, a person signals unavailability.

# SECTION 4 - PUTTING OTHERS AT EASE AND BUILDING RAPPORT

**SECTION 4 - Putting Others at Ease and Building Rapport**

Good reception during conversation puts people at ease and increases your approachability. To provide this, you need to stop what you are doing and pay full attention, make people feel good about conversations they have with you, and ask appropriate questions. To help ensure that people enjoy conversations with you, you can give appropriate compliments, show genuine interest in people, be pleasant and polite, and be patient with people's foibles and anxieties.

One aspect of improving your approachability is developing rapport with others. Rapport enhances your approachability and is built by listening actively, harmonizing with others, and sharing your thoughts and feelings.

# PUTTING OTHERS AT EASE

**Putting others at ease**

Once you have gone to the effort to make contact or to invite contact, what else can you do to improve your approachability? Your reception of other people – the behaviors you use when actually speaking to them – can have an important impact on how approachable they consider you to be.

People remember previous encounters they had with you, and generally find you easier to approach if they remember feeling comfortable with you. So depending on how well you interact with people, they could either look forward to talking with you or shrink from future encounters. It's very important that your conversations with people help them to feel accepted, relaxed, and engaged.

**Recommendations for setting people at ease**

A comfortable conversation is one you enjoy or find satisfying and in which you feel genuinely listened to. If you're having a discussion with someone who's preoccupied or not paying real attention, you don't feel comfortable expressing yourself.

If someone is paying attention but is rude or judgmental, you won't feel comfortable talking with that person. If someone is merely polite but doesn't make you feel welcome and appreciated, it's still hard to interact. You need to feel nurtured in some way to truly be set at ease by another person – even if you know this person well.

One of your goals should be to put people at ease. Setting people at ease is an active and ongoing process, even with individuals who know you well. So when people speak with you, you need to be proactive in making them feel comfortable.

The first thing you can do when a colleague approaches you is to stop what you're doing and pay attention. If you're busy with other tasks, you can't pay proper attention and people may feel as if they are intruding or interrupting you. If people approach you when you are too busy to attend to them, arrange to meet with them later.

If you have to stop or postpone a conversation to attend to something urgent, most people will understand. However, it's important that you promise to get back to your colleague later and that you keep your word.

Something else you can do to make colleagues feel at ease is to make them feel good about a conversation you're having. This involves using appropriate compliments, showing genuine interest, being patient, and being pleasant and polite.

**Compliment appropriately**

People like getting compliments, especially ones that give them a chance to talk about themselves. Compliments can convey caring and show that you notice and appreciate a colleague's good qualities or work.

However, not all compliments are comfortable to receive. Getting too personal is inappropriate. For example, complimenting a person on the color of her eyes might be seen as making a pass or simply be too intimate. Complimenting a new hairdo, on the other hand, shows that you notice the care that she has taken with her appearance. Insincere compliments give a bad impression. If you compliment someone on an achievement but you're not truly impressed, you may come across as insincere – and that makes people uncomfortable.

**Show genuine interest**

As much as possible, be genuinely interested in what people have to say. Most people enjoy conversations about absorbing topics with a good listener who shares their enthusiasm. The best way to be genuinely interested in what a person has to say is to find a topic that both of you enjoy talking about.

**Be patient**

Everybody has flaws they feel self-conscious about. Almost everyone has some anxiety about work or personal issues. To set people at ease, you need to be patient with their foibles and anxieties. Offering empathy and gentle reassurances can alleviate worries, as can working through problems rather than offering unsolicited personal advice.

**Be pleasant and polite**

To be pleasant and polite, aim to convey respect, warmth, and consideration toward your colleagues. Always smile and greet people. It may also be appropriate to shake hands, offer a seat, or thank someone for coming by. Offering tea or coffee and beginning a conversation with a little small talk is another way to set people at ease.

Neela works at a large accounting firm. A new employee, William, approaches her with a question. Follow along as she converses with William.

**William:** Hi, Neela. How are you?

*William seems nervous and shy.*

**Neela:** Busy as always, William. I heard the boss praising your efficiency the other day. That must be nice.

*Neela sounds insincere.*

**William:** Yeah, everyone around here seems to be overrun with work. Honestly, I find it quite hard to keep up sometimes, but people have been very understanding.

*William seems uncomfortable.*

**Neela:** Oh really? I thought from the boss's comment that you must be on top of things by now.

*Neela's tone of voice lacks sincerity.*

**William:** Well, I have a lot to learn. Listen, I wanted to ask you if you know why the May 18 entry is missing from the Gordon file. I can't find it anywhere.

*William still seems uncomfortable.*

**Neela:** Is it missing?! Oh, that must be because Henry didn't transfer the data on Friday. Now why didn't I notice that?

*Neela looks at William in surprise.*

**William:** OK, I'll take it up with Henry. Thanks, Neela.

*William is still uncomfortable.*

**Neela:** Don't mention it.

*Neela gets back to work.*

Was Neela successful in putting William at ease? No, he remained uncomfortable throughout the conversation, and no wonder! From the start, Neela neglected to give William her full attention, treat him pleasantly, or even greet him politely. She continued to focus on her work and showed little interest in what he had to say.

Instead of empathizing patiently with William's expressions of awkwardness on a new job, she disregarded his feelings. Her attempts at compliments were insincere, and she missed a chance to praise William for catching a data entry omission. Instead, she focused on herself.

In the future, William is unlikely to approach Neela again if he doesn't have to. Another way to put others at ease is to ask questions. Asking questions gives people the opportunity to share information with you and can show genuine interest, indicating that you want to listen and learn more.

Not all types of questions work equally well in conversation. To keep a conversation moving and convey interest, you should choose open-ended questions over closed-ended questions, and choose follow-up questions over empty questions.

**Open-ended questions versus closed-ended questions**

Closed-ended questions elicit just a "yes" or "no" or another very brief answer. For example, if you ask "Are you enjoying your new role?" your colleague can answer this with a simple "yes" or "no."

Open-ended questions kindle conversation by encouraging the other person to elaborate. For instance, if you ask "How are you finding your new role?" you encourage your colleague to elaborate when answering the question. Open-ended questions work best for keeping a discussion going.

**Follow-up questions versus empty questions**

In casual conversation, people often ask questions simply out of habit, when in reality they have little interest in the answer. "How's it going?" or "What's new?" are examples of these questions. They're often asked out of politeness, and they usually don't convey sincere interest. Questions asked merely for the sake of talking don't set people at ease and can annoy them instead.

Follow-up questions, on the other hand, help you to learn more about what's being said. A follow-up question is one that relates to something another person has said, or something you know they are involved in. "What projects are you moving on to after we finish with the Smith account?" would convey more sincere interest than "So...what's new?"

Sara works at the same accounting company as William and Neela. William is hesitant to bother Neela again, so he approaches Sara with a question. Follow along as she tries to help him feel more at ease.

**William:** Hi, Sara.

*William seems uncertain.*

**Sara:** Hi there William. I've heard that you're settling in well, though you must have had a busy month. What can I do for you?

*Sara has turned away from her computer and is smiling at William.*

**William:** Yeah, I've learned a lot this month! I wanted to see you because I need some advice on the Gibson account. I'm feeling a bit confused about the taxable and non-taxable expenses.

*William seems stressed and worried.*

**Sara:** It can sometimes be confusing to work out which expenses are deductible. Which ones are you unsure of?

*Sara is looking at William patiently and warmly.*

**William:** Well, some of the study expenses don't really look deductible to me. They want to deduct for one employee's art classes.

*William seems calmer.*

**Sara:** OK. That's a very good question. Well done for picking that up! Why would they include this as a deductible business expense?

*Sara is nodding and smiling.*

**William:** Well, maybe they need to work on design projects. I'm really not sure. That's the problem. There isn't enough information here.

*William is now looking absorbed and not self-conscious.*

Sara did a number of things to put William at ease and make him feel good about the conversation. She stopped what she was doing when William approached her. She asked meaningful, open-ended questions that followed on from points of discussion and showed an interest in William's experience with the company. She was patient with William's anxieties and complimented him for his attention to detail.

Although Sara did a fairly good job of setting William at ease, she failed to offer him a seat or thank him for approaching her for advice. These acts of politeness and invitation could have helped him to feel more welcome and less nervous about speaking with her. Sara was pleasant and warm, but her approach could still be improved.

**Question**

## Interpersonal Communication

Which statements are likely to put someone else at ease and therefore help to facilitate conversation?

**Options:**

1. What beautiful flowers you have on your desk. They brighten the whole room.
2. I loved your new marketing idea. I'm such a fan of dogs. What was your inspiration?
3. Please, take a seat. I have time.
4. That's quite alright. We all make mistakes, believe me!
5. I landed this job right after I completed my Ph.D. at Yale.
6. You have such gorgeous, long eyelashes.

**Answer:**

Option 1: This option is correct. This compliment isn't too personal and gives the other person a chance to talk about the flowers. This will help set him at ease and facilitate conversation.

Option 2: This option is correct. By showing enthusiasm and asking for more details about someone's ideas, you demonstrate genuine interest and facilitate conversation. Also, by asking an open-ended question, you encourage further discussion.

Option 3: This option is correct. Asking someone to be seated is polite, and assuring that person you're available will put her at ease.

Option 4: This option is correct. By being patient with a person's faults and showing you understand his anxieties, you allay that person's fears and help him to feel comfortable.

Option 5: This option is incorrect. Listing your achievements without providing any interesting details doesn't facilitate conversation or set other people at ease.

Option 6: This option is incorrect. This compliment is too personal and could unsettle the person it's given to. Responding to this compliment would be difficult, so it doesn't facilitate conversation either.

# LISTENING

**Listening**

Another goal of reception is to build rapport with people. Rapport is a much deeper connection than simply getting to know people and being able to set them at ease. So what is rapport and how do you build it?

When rapport exists between people, they have a deeply harmonious and sympathetic relationship or connection. Once a connection has been made, a relationship forged, and trust developed between people, rapport may then be built over time. Initial connection, trust, and a relationship are all prerequisites for rapport, but rapport is a deeper bond than these three. Rapport is more intimate and more friendly.

Three key techniques can help you build rapport with another person:
- listen,
- harmonize, and
- share.

Listening in order to build rapport is not a passive or simple process. It's an activity that requires close attention to another person and to what this person is saying. Active listening requires that you eliminate all distractions and focus exclusively on the speaker. You listen closely for both the meaning and intent of the message, all the while controlling your own emotional reactions. Finally, you ask questions to clarify the message and summarize it to verify that you've understood.

**Eliminate distractions**

To listen to someone properly, you need to eliminate distractions. Try to structure your environment to avoid being distracted – find a place to talk where you will not be disturbed during your conversation. Put down anything you are holding at the time, face the other person, and put your calls on hold so you can concentrate better.

**Focus on the speaker**

Focus on the speaker and demonstrate your focus by maintaining appropriate eye contact, glancing away from the speaker only from time to time. This shows the person that he has your attention. It also allows you to notice the person's body language, expressions, and gestures so that you can better understand what is communicated to you and how the speaker feels.

**Listen for meaning and intent**

When you listen to someone, you need to listen not only to the person's words but also to what the person means by them. What is she really trying to say and why? Often people convey multiple ideas, thoughts, and feelings when talking. So you need to pay attention to tone of voice and how they deliver their messages.

**Control your emotions**

Sometimes it's upsetting to listen to people who are agitated, disagreeable, or have said something that is offensive to you. If you react emotionally without hearing a person out, you stop listening attentively. You can easily misunderstand the message and the motive for it. So when you listen actively, try to remain calm and put your personal feelings aside as much as possible.

**Ask questions**

Because meaning is often subtle and words can be unclear, it's important to ask questions to clarify what a person is saying. Asking questions is essential to active listening. You also ask questions to continue the conversation, to deepen your understanding, and to show the other person that you want to learn more.

**Summarize**

Summarizing the meaning and intent of what someone has said confirms that you have understood. By restating key points, you demonstrate to the speaker you've grasped the essence of what he's saying, and you give this person an opportunity to correct your misinterpretations. Summarizing the intent of someone's words both clarifies and shows recognition of their feelings and motivations.

**Question**

How easy do you find it to listen actively to people when you don't agree with what they're saying?

**Options:**

1. Fairly easy
2. Not very easy
3. Very difficult

**Answer:**

Option 1: Being able to listen actively to people you disagree with is a good indication you can control your emotional reactions. How can you further develop your ability to understand and accept other people and what they communicate to you?

Option 2: Perhaps you sometimes react emotionally to what people say. It may help to remember to stay calm or to listen with the deliberate intent to understand better. In this way, you may find common ground with others and be less disturbed by their differences in perspective.

Option 3: You probably have strong emotional reactions to what people say. Try to stay calm and focus on people's motives for communicating. In this way, you'll better be able to understand their perspectives and tolerate differences. It may be helpful to voice your disagreement in a nonconfrontational way.

Disagreement need not be a barrier to rapport. Your intention should be to understand and recognize other people's viewpoints and ideas – not necessarily to agree with them. Rapport is not likely to be threatened by disagreements, but rather by common listening mistakes. These mistakes include finishing people's sentences for them or cutting people off while they're talking.

If you daydream or pretend to listen when you're actually thinking of something else, this damages rapport and hampers conversation. If you avoid people because you don't want to listen to them, this also prevents you from building rapport with them.

# HARMONIZING AND SHARING

**Harmonizing and sharing**

To build rapport, you need not only to listen actively but also to harmonize. Creating harmony is a process of matching your understanding, behavior, body language, and interests with those of others. By synchronizing yourself with other people, you create a sense of unity and companionship. Consider how others probably see things and focus your efforts appropriately. Empathy is generated through this common accord, and this builds rapport.

To harmonize with others, you need to find common ground and match your understanding with them. To do this, find out what perspectives, goals, and interests you have in common, and let others know that you share them. Matching others' behavior and body language to harmonize with them isn't a direct mimicking process. It's something that often happens naturally and easily when you're aware of those around you and you're responsive to them.

To enhance your ability to match and thereby harmonize with others, pay attention to how they are moving and their tones of voice. Then allow yourself to mirror this behavior without identically matching each gesture or inflection. For example, if a colleague is leaning forward and speaking slowly with a serious tone, try leaning forward a little. Avoid using a playful tone because this will undermine the seriousness of your colleague's message.

Sharing information about yourself and how you feel allows others to get to know more about who you are. And, as others understand you more, they tend to feel more comfortable and more free to share information about themselves. This provides a good foundation for building rapport.

To share with others and build rapport, you should be prepared to volunteer information and answer reasonable questions about your life, feelings, and interests. Let people know what you are interested in so that they can learn more about you and find common ground with you. If you don't share with others, they may find you secretive and aloof. This will damage your rapport – they're more likely to feel guarded and nervous around you.

**Question**

Which examples are possible ways of building rapport?

**Options:**

1. Leaning against a wall to chat with others who are also doing so

2. Mentioning how proud you are that your child won an award at school

3. Turning your back to your computer when holding a discussion with a colleague

4. Laughing when your companion laughs during a conversation

5. Shaking someone's hand when you're introduced

6. Helping a colleague express himself better by saying something that he's struggling to articulate

**Answer:**

Option 1: This is a correct option. By mirroring the postures of people you talk to, you harmonize yourself with them and help to build rapport.

Option 2: This is a correct option. By sharing your pride in your child's achievement, you give others a chance to get to know you, helping to generate rapport with them.

Option 3: This is a correct option. By turning your back to your computer, you can avoid being distracted from your colleague and the conversation. This will help you to listen more actively, helping to create better rapport.

Option 4: This is a correct option. By matching your companion's good humor when interacting, you create harmony and rapport.

Option 5: This is an incorrect option. Although politeness enhances your approachability by putting others at ease, it doesn't necessarily help to build rapport.

Option 6: This is an incorrect option. Saying things for other people who are trying to speak for themselves doesn't build rapport. It demonstrates a failure to listen actively.

# REFERENCES

**References**
- **Powerful Communication Skills: How to Communicate with Confidence** - 1998, Colleen McKenna, Career Press
- **Trust & Betrayal in the Workplace: Building Effective Relationships in Your Organization** - 2006, Dennis S. Reina and Michelle L. Reina Berrett, Koehler Publishers
- **The Etiquette Edge: The Unspoken Rules for Business Success** - 2005, Beverly Langford, AMACOM
- **Communication Skills for Managers** - 2002, Janis Fisher Chan, AMACOM
- **Effective Communications for Project Management** - 2008, Ralph L. Kliem, Auerbach Publications
- **Communications Skills for Project Managers** - 2009, G. Michael Campbell, AMACOM

Interpersonal Communication

- **Getting Your Message Across: Communication Skills for Managers, Fifth Edition** - 2002, Janis Fisher Chan, AMACOM
- **The Million Dollar Toolbox: A Blueprint for Transforming Your Life & Your Career With Powerful Communication Skills** - 2001, Ty Boyd, Alexa Press
- **Communication in the Workplace** - 2007, Baden Eunson, John Wiley & Sons
- **Interpersonal Communication: Questioning, Listening, and Feedback Skills** - 2005, Tony Alessandra and Phillip L. Hunsaker, Tony Alessandra
- **Listening Attentively** - 2005, Tony Alessandra, Tony Alessandra
- **Active Listening: Improve Your Ability to Listen and Lead** - 2006, Michael H. Hoppe, Center for Creative Leadership
- **Developing Positive Assertiveness, Third Edition** - 2002, Sam R. Lloyd, Crisp Learning
- **Emotional Capitalists: The New Leaders: Essential Strategies for Building Your Emotional Intelligence and Leadership Success** - 2007, Martyn Newman, John Wiley & Sons
- **Stop Pushing Me Around!: A Workplace Guide for the Timid, Shy, and Less Assertive** - 2006, Ilise Benun, Career Press
- **Getting Real: 10 Truth Skills You Need to Live an Authentic Life** - 2001, Susan Campbell, New World Library

Sorin Dumitrascu

- **Confessions from the Corner Office: 15 Instincts That Will Help You Get There** - 2007, Scott Aylward and Pattye Moore, John Wiley & Sons
- **The 108 Skills of Natural Born Leaders** - 2001, Warren Blank, AMACOM
- **Communication Excellence: Using NLP to Supercharge Your Business Skills** - 2000, Ian R. McLaren, Crown House Publishing
-

# GLOSSARY

**Glossary**
**A**

**active listening** - A listening technique where you listen for both factual content and intent and use questions and summarizing to clarify what you hear.

**aggressive behavior** - Behavior that is rude and abrupt, insensitive of others' views, disrespectful, or pushy.

**assertive behavior** - Behavior that is honest and direct, and that involves standing up for certain views or rights while maintaining respect for others.

**availability** - An element of approachability where you ensure you are physically and personally available to others.

**B**

**body language** - Nonverbal communication through physical characteristics such as posture, facial expression, eye contact, hand gestures, and tone and volume of voice. Used to communicate a person's enthusiasm, attentiveness, or willingness to listen to the other party.

**C**

**closed-ended question** - A question requiring one of a limited set of possible answers, such as "yes" or "no." It's useful for clarifying specific points or confirming understanding of what a speaker has said.

**communicating productively** - Giving feedback with the aim of a positive or constructive outcome.

**communication** - The sharing or transmission of ideas, thoughts, or feelings between people.

**communication model** - The components that make up the process of communication, along with the way these components interact. The basic communication model consists of five components — sender and receiver; medium; contextual factors; message; and feedback.

**confident behavior** - The actions and mannerisms that project confidence to others, including body language and vocalization.

**constructive criticism** - The feedback you give people in order to improve their work or behavior.

**contextual factors** - In relation to communication, factors associated with the context in which a message is sent and received. Examples are body language, timing, and the environment or setting in which communication occurs. These variables influence the effectiveness of communication.

**credibility** - The objective assessment that another person is believable and convincing.

**E**

**evaluative listening** - A type of listening characterized by the listener paying attention to the words spoken, but not the body language accompanying them.

**F**

**fact feedback** - Feedback used to clarify or demonstrate understanding of the factual content of a speaker's message.

**feedback** - A response to a communicated message. Feedback is itself essentially a message, and can take verbal, visual, or written forms.

**feeling feedback** - Feedback about the emotions or feelings conveyed in a speaker's message.

**H**

**harmonizing** - A process of matching your understanding, behavior, body language, and interests with those of others.

**hearing** - The passive process of registering sounds.

**I**

**indexing** - The process of ordering information by outlining main points and subpoints.

**inflection** - The rise and fall of the pitch of your voice during speech.

**interpersonal communication** - Interaction and sharing of ideas between small numbers of people in close physical proximity.

**J**

**jargon** - Specialist terminology that is difficult to understand.

**L**

**listening** - The active process of interpreting what has been heard.

**M**

**medium** - In relation to communication, the means by which a message is delivered. Common examples include face-to-face conversations, e-mail, instant messages, telephone calls, and letters.

**message** - The object of communication or the thing that is being communicated. A message may take a number of forms, including spoken, written, visual, and physical signal. Some qualities of a message include its wording, directness, and purpose.

**mixed message** - A message sent by a speaker in which the speaker's body language contradicts the words he or she is saying.

**N**

**noise** - Anything that causes a receiver to fail to receive the message a sender intends to communicate correctly. Examples include distracting sounds, mispronunciation, and errors that occur during message transmission.

**O**

**open-ended question** - A question that requires more than a specific, short answer such as "yes" or "no." It encourages a speaker to elaborate.

**P**

**paraphrase** - To summarize or repeat a message in your own words.

**passive behavior** - Behavior that is submissive, characterized by a lack of confidence and difficulty in engaging in group discussions.

**passive listening** - A type of listening in which the listener fails to engage actively with the speaker and doesn't provide the speaker with any feedback. Passive listening doesn't facilitate effective communication.

**passive-aggressive behavior** - Behavior that is secretively aggressive but avoids actual confrontation.

**posture** - The way you carry yourself.

**R**

**rapport** - A meaningful and harmonious relationship.

**reaching out** - An element of approachability where you proactively initiate contact and welcome new relationships.

**receiver** - The person or entity that is receiving the message.

**reception** - An element of approachability where you remain open and attentive during communication with a person so that person feels confident, comfortable, and understood. This is achieved by putting people at ease, listening, harmonizing, and sharing.

**red flag** - A word or topic that evokes a strong emotional reaction in the listener.

**S**

**self-talk** - Internal communication or what you tell yourself within the privacy of your own mind.

**speed gap** - The difference between the speed at which people can speak and the speed at which they can think. Generally, people can think three to four times faster than they can talk.

**summarizing** - An active listening technique where you summarize key points and the intent of a message to ensure you understand what has been said.

**T**

**targeted message** - A message that is tailored to communicate most effectively with a specific receiver. A targeted message takes into account factors like the receiver's preferences, interests and knowledge level; the context in which the receiver receives the message, the timing of the message, and feedback required as a result of the message.

**tone** - The indication of your feelings in your voice.

**trust** - The subjective feeling that another person has good intentions, is being open and honest with you, and is safe to interact with.

**V**

**vocalization** - The way you use your voice to make sounds.

www.ingramcontent.com/pod-product-compliance
Lightning Source LLC
Chambersburg PA
CBHW020859180526
45163CB00007B/2564